SOUTHERN HARVEST

SOUTHERN HARVEST

written and engraved by Clare Leighton

with a foreword by Janet Lembke

THE UNIVERSITY OF GEORGIA PRESS

Athens and London

Published in 1997 by the University of Georgia Press, Athens, Georgia 30602
Foreword © 1997 by the University of Georgia Press
Set in Plantin
The paper in this book meets the guidelines for permanence and durability
of the Committee onProduction Guidelines for Book Longevity of the
Council on Library Resources.

Printed in the United States of America

01 00 99 98 97   C   5   4   3   2   1

Library of Congress Cataloging in Publication Data
Leighton, Clare, 1899-1989.
Southern harvest / by Clare Leighton ; with engravings by the author.
p. cm.
Originally published : New York : Macmillan, 1942.
ISBN 0-8203-1948-1 (alk. paper)
1. Southern States—Description and travel.
2. Southern States—Social life and customs—1865-
3. Agriculture—Southern States—History—19th century.
4. Agriculture—Southern States—History—20th century. I. Title.
F215.L5 1997   97-16773
975—dc21

British Library Cataloging in Publication Data available

Southern Harvest was first published by the Macmillan Company in 1942.

FOREWORD

Janet Lembke

CORNCRIBS, streamside mills with working water wheels, draught horses and mules plodding patiently down furrows, and floodwaters surging with sudden force down a mountain river—I remember these from my earliest years. I remember southern voices, my father's among them, saying "yoes" when they spoke of the ewes that grazed in their pastures, bore lambs—often twins—each spring, and finally ended as mutton on the dinner table. I remember the communal efforts on my father's farm, come November and its sharp, crisp days, to butcher the big hogs that had been roughed through on pasture summerlong, then penned and fattened on corn six weeks before the busy, bloody day. And I remember the Saturday gatherings of country people not just in my town's courthouse square but also up and down its five-block Main Street; this was the time of World War II, and to keep its female students safe from unruliness and worse, my school gave us freedom on Mondays but commanded Saturday attendance.

I remember these things vividly now, but they'd been tucked away till Clare Leighton reminded me.

Clare Leighton's *Southern Harvest*, first published in 1942, celebrates rural life throughout the Southeast. The venues for her stories are Virginia, the Carolinas, and Tennessee, Georgia, Alabama, Mississippi, and Louisiana (merely calling this roll of states coaxes the tongue into a drawl). The acts and events she tells about are those intimately connected with fertile earth and the circling of the seasons: picking cotton, growing and auctioning tobacco, killing hogs, and pressing out sorghum's "long sweetnin'" in a primitive, mule-driven mill, a mill no different from those used immemorially in the

v

Mediterranean and the Middle East. Two of the stories are fiction—"written in the third person," as the author puts it. One deals with the terror and courage provoked by an unexpected flood, the other with the sad misperceptions of an impoverished plantation owner who opens his once grand house to the public and stands an old black employee "in the road like a pimp to catch strangers." But both short stories possess truth as powerful as that of the essays.

The people Leighton celebrates throughout are mainly field hands and mountain men, the poorest of the rural poor. The assembly in the courthouse square of every southern county seat on each and every Saturday consists of "these people, these leaning, lounging men in their blue jeans, these gossiping women in their clean shabby prints, these Negroes with their look of unrest, these small thin children with flaxen hair and bare feet."

But times have changed. The twentieth century reels toward its close; technology has transformed the Western world. News leaps across the planet, agribusiness delivers our daily bread, men have walked on the moon, and caution (abetted perhaps by an urge toward political correctness) dictates "African American" instead of the words Leighton uses—"Negro," "colored," and "pickaninny." Here, excusably, she uses the vocabulary of her era; she does not use it to patronize those less fortunate, not even in the unwitting fashion that mars some memoirs contemporary with hers, like Marjorie Kinnan Rawlings's *Cross Creek*. "I have seen the truth," Leighton writes of the burdened, weary black cotton-pickers, "for I have seen man in servitude to a plant." And in an old black woman, caught in a limbo between slavery and the exercise of freedom, she sees "the tragedy of a mighty race problem," a problem that persists today.

But what good to us here and now are these stories told more than fifty years ago, stories that deal with stoop labor, sweat, superstition, and poverty?

She herself provides more than one answer. Battered by news of war, the world shaken and scorched by bombs, she turns her eyes to the mountains of western North Carolina and thinks of St. Paul's discovery of joy and peace as he listens to mountains and hills breaking into song. She writes, "We can read something, and with our eyes and our lips and our brains we follow the words; but as Paul's revelation came to him unheralded, so we can never know at what exact moment words we read may flame into meaning." In the same way, then, these stories may ignite some new understanding of our human condition.

A vague and exaggerated notion? Not at all.

To begin with, *Southern Harvest* is an adventure story. Like a passenger on the *Mayflower*, like the people stolen in Africa and shipped across the sea, like Aeneas braving unknown territory after Troy's defeat, Leighton left behind her native England and migrated west to a new, strange land. She did not know if she would find welcome here, or ease of spirit, but learned through traveling, listening, and writing about the lives she encountered that she could indeed be homesick. The homesickness was not, however, for England but "for a people and country I had never seen"—the country of the American South. The secret of coming home to an unfamiliar place lay in discovering "one unfailing softener of nostalgia . . . the universality of the things of the earth." Many aspects of this unexpected homecoming are illustrated by her own handsome woodcuts—mills and mountain flowers, a woman lifting a cotton sack, men hefting hands of tobacco in a packing barn. And, like a medieval manuscript, each chapter bears an initial letter illuminated by a careful cut.

Clare Leighton brings a splendid, kinetic vigor to the account of her newfound world. Imagination and precision invest her images. Rain falls "like a tent of wet steel." Mist lies "heavy like a woolen scarf." A certain slant of light on the live oaks "turns Spanish moss to smoke." The summer sun beats ever relentlessly upon the land; "the hard black buckshot earth resists all touch," "the air is filled with the hot smell of scorching hooves from the mules' feet," and the "stingy shadow of a fence" offers no relief to man or beast. (If another writer is able so well to use mere words about heat to produce real sweat and torpor, I don't know who it is.) And the people who toil, toting long white sacks, in the sun-hammered cotton fields are "butterflies bound to earth by constricting white cocoons." The rush of water and the creaking, grinding sounds of mills rise audibly from the pages, as does the rapid, bubbling cry of the tobacco auctioneer and the mountain man's plaintive, dulcimer-accompanied song. Even better, without help from anything but her own keen ear, she has captured the rhythms and the regional variations in human speech. Over here, the Reverend Hill speaks with devout horror about his encounter with the Devil, a moment that is also pictured in a woodcut; over there, a "po' white" in an Appalachian cove softly, gently gives the reasons that his family lost its land. Corn-shuckers gossip; at the auction barn, a farmer tells how brightleaf tobacco is cured and graded—and brags some on his crop. And yonder, amid wood smoke and trees stripped by autumn of their leaves, men and women engage in necessary reminiscence about hogs and Novembers past as they go about slaughtering and dressing out old Betty.

"Necessary" is the vital word. For, like every task in rural life, the killing of a hog is not a purely secular activity. Rather, it is connected to all that is holy and unseen. Leighton subscribes to the ancient view, known by heart to the classical Greeks, that all things in heaven and earth are aspects of the divine. The old, lame, stoop-shouldered miller, whom she watches at work in a disappearing trade, seems "in tune with the mythology of earth," and the man himself has "bridged the division between human and tree and earth."

More than that, working the soil and participating in "the magic of harvest" (her phrase) constitute a form of liturgy. The language of the stories constantly emphasizes Leighton's perception that "one of the strongest things in the whole world is the sense of earth ritual." The milling of sorghum is followed by a ceremony, a "sacramental" tasting of the hot liquid poured over fresh-baked biscuits. The people assembled on Saturdays in the courthouse square are seen as congregants, each making an "offering of his single identity upon the communal altar of life." At the hog-killing, every participant is priest or acolyte, from the man who shoots the hog and the man who keeps the fire going under the scalding barrel to the women who dress out the pig and carry away its steaming liver for the common feast. And all of them move with tenderness, reverence, and a "deep sense of ritual" through a timeless "sacrificial rite." Like the ancient Greeks, like traditional people everywhere, Leighton knows that strength comes from touching earth. She knows, too, that humankind's hope for sanity lies in "ordered obedience to the seasons." I'm sure she's right.

But where is hope for our time? More than half a century has slid away since Leighton committed her beliefs to paper. Today, many of us who live in the industrialized world are separated by layers of concrete, metal, and plastic from contact with earth. I am lucky enough, and old enough, to have lived on a family farm and to remember raw milk that tasted of onion grass in the spring, the salted hams curing in the attic, breakfast eggs that I'd collected from the hens, and alfalfa brought to the barn on a wagon pulled by huge horses, then pitched by human muscle into the high, fragrant loft where there were always barnswallows and a kindle of kittens. Today, however, most of us may be irremediably dispossessed.

Yet, we do have ways to reconnect, to come home, as Clare Leighton did, to a place we've never been. Reading *Southern Harvest* is one of them.

INTRODUCTION

SOME BOOKS are written for the problematic public to read. Others are written for the sake of the writer, out of his own special need. I think I can truthfully say that this book of mine falls into the second category. *Southern Harvest* is my endeavor to push my roots into their new earth of this American continent. For, as in England and in Europe my true happiness lay always among the people of the earth, rather than in cities, here the same thing would be true, I knew. There is a universality about the people of the earth that is healing, and it matters little whether one be talking with a tobacco farmer in North Carolina or a plowman in Devonshire. So, I knew, my sole chance of adjustment over here, in the country of my adoption, and my best cure for the incomparable fret of nostalgia as well as my only hope for becoming one with my new land, would be to wander around among the workers on this earth and learn their habits and their lore.

This book is the result.

Being an Englishwoman, I feel that I have especial need for an *apologia*. Of all the sinners who go to foreign countries and on the scrappiest of acquaintances deem themselves worthy to write about them, we English are probably the worst. We are supposed to carry around with us an arrogance, in the light of which we are able to understand all peoples and all countries. For this reason I feel apologetic about writing this book at all. My sole defence is that I have never pretended that it is a knowledgeable book. It makes no statement. It preaches no lesson. It is simply the impressions of one who has wandered over the South through several years, loving it and its people and seeing fundamentally little difference between them and the tillers of the soil of my own English countryside.

Needing to live close to the land, I forsook the cities of America and, before I knew what was happening, I found myself friendly towards and accepted by the people who worked the American scene.

If I had lived longer among them it is probable that I should have feared to write of them at all, for I should have begun truly to know them. Even as it is, I had to hasten with this book, before timidity should too much overtake me. For there are two ways of approaching creation: from the one vantage point of excitement in an entirely new world, and from the other vantage point of complete understanding. The tremendous excitement I felt when I first saw a tobacco barn, or heard the colored cotton pickers singing in the fields of the Mississippi Delta begins imperceptibly to merge now into the identification of myself with all around me, even as I can feel the power of the American earth nourishing the roots that I have transplanted. "You will probably write two books," an American publisher once said to me. "The first one will be created out of your initial excitement, and the next one will be after many, many years, when timidity leaves you and knowledge takes its place."

And so I make no excuses for writing this book; but if I have chanced upon some new excitement to give to the American people about its own world I am glad. I have never said, "This is the South," but only, "I have seen this." I do not aim at an inclusive presentation of the South. With the exception of two stories written in the third person, FLOOD and LOUISIANA PILGRIMAGE, these chapters are personal impressions. I merely record my excitements and my delights.

CLARE LEIGHTON

Baltimore, Maryland, 1940
Chapel Hill, North Carolina, July, 1942.

CONTENTS

SOUTHERN HARVEST

COTTON

WHAT is it that they make me think of, these cotton pickers in the Mississippi Delta? Is it of some great wounded insects, their damaged wings drooped and dragged upon the ground? But no; that is more the picture I had of the cotton pickers of North Carolina, with the shabby tow sacks looped over their backs and across their shoulders. Here in the Delta country, where the sacks are long and white like enormous pillowcases, here it is something else that I am reminded of. And then it comes to me; it is a field of garish butterflies I look upon, of butterflies bound to earth by constricting white cocoons, butterflies straining in vain to emerge and fly. This must be why there is such pathos in cotton pickers: they are dragged to earth by the heavy pick sacks, unable to soar.

Feeling this, I know that I watch a world of symbols, and the great sacks that hold these people to the earth bind them in many ways. I know that I watch struggle made manifest: tug and lift to the skies, pull and drag to the earth. But always the sack triumphs—triumphing the more, the fuller it is. I see that man over there, bent to the earth, and it is as though the curves and shapes before me are eloquent as no words or thoughts can be. The curve runs from head and back, into the half-filled sack that ties him to earth; and as I watch him, weighed down by this sack to this earth, black as his very skin, hard as his skull, the small head lifts itself towards the skies in a shout of praise. What is it that he can praise? Listening, I hear him sing his jubilation to the Lord God.

Thirty-nine colored folks in this cotton-picking gang move along the rows, thirty-nine backs bend, thirty-nine pairs of feet drag the great white sacks behind them. And as they move slowly across this unending sea of cotton, it is as though a host of locusts were consuming everything in their passage, and the white surface melts before them, leaving green of leaf and nothing stirring except the multitudinous grasshoppers, leaping among the stalks.

How small they seem, these pickers, against this vast ocean of cotton before them! The plain stretches as far as eye can see, away and away, over unbelievable flatness, that is broken only by a Negro shack or a cotton house at the rim of the field. Somewhere beyond vision, at the far horizon, dark-leaved, dripping trees border the Mississippi, and an upright column of smoke proclaims the passing of a river steamer, the sound of its whistle deep-throated over the absolute flatness.

For though the river may be far away, beyond the distant edge of the cotton fields, always it is present in the mind, an unappeasable, arbitrary force that tosses up here an island of rich alluvial soil upon which the trees grow with magical speed, and submerges there a tongue of land that holds the sum of one man's harvest. In caprice it changes the map of the countryside within the sprouting of a season, caring nothing for man and his patient plowing and sowing.

But it is September now, and the river is low in its banks. Heat and drought spread over the land. The hard black buckshot earth resists all touch, and feet as dark as the earth they tread sting and ache through gaping uppers and worn-away shoe soles. Mile upon mile of blistering earth, and even the laden cotton stalks fail to give shade to the path that the feet must tread. Relentless heat beats down from the colorless sky, and meets the accumulated heat of summer that strikes up from the earth. The pickers are caught between heat of sky and heat of earth, and there is no escape. The violent black soil swings from extreme to extreme. What would they not give today, this gang of pickers, if feet could wade and sink into the cool black mud of early spring? Hitting my own feet against the brutal buckshot

4

earth, I think of the day that I first saw this Delta country, with the sipe water lying over the land beyond the levee and the feeling of spring gay in the air. Mules gambolled in the gentle sunshine, and

the smooth, ridged earthworks of the levee were sprinkled with little magenta flowers. Over the land the black fields lay empty and wait-ing, waiting for the spring sunshine to warm the earth, that the cot-ton might be planted. But the March sun was as yet too weak, and across the cutover land, the turnout land, the plowed cotton fields, mist lay heavy like a woolen scarf, and charred tree stumps were doubled in the swollen drainage ditches. It is not easy to think of it as the same world I tread now, under the burning sky, upon blister-ing earth. The levee camps were alert then, and eyes turned ever towards the flood gauge. And over the frighteningly wide stretch of empty field before me moved twelve sets of plows and mules, like slow shuttles across a black-warped loom.

They are singing now, these pickers, and the color of their voices is rich as their skin, or as the earth they tread. But while they sing, releasing their sack-bound spirit into the quivering heat of the air, the sounds turn into a moan. I look towards Clarence Lucky, the great Negro in the streaming pennants of rags that seem all the time as though they would catch into the burrs of the cotton and be torn from him, clearing his classic body of clutter, and suddenly I know what it is I hear. For Clarence Lucky's mother-in-law, Full Bosom Jefferson, died a week ago and, though she has been duly buried, the funeral will not take place until after the cotton harvest, when there will be enough money to buy new clothes for the occasion. Clarence and his wife Rebecca drag their stubbed feet over the burning earth, and bend their backs to the picking of cotton with doubled vigor, that the ceremony may be worthy of Full Bosom Jefferson. And so, as he treads his row and picks his cotton, he is teaching his children to moan, and before the sun has sunk low enough to throw the shadows of the pickers across the width of more than two rows of cotton the children will have learnt their responds and will be able to sing and answer in unison: Pencil McKinney, Cream-Cheese-and-Celery, Peg-with-Peg-Leg and little Ebenezer, these small ragged colored creatures that sit as they pick, and drag their miniature sacks behind them, obediently moan and chant over their work. And when the great black giant Clarence Lucky empties his children's little gatherings into his own sack, it is to the rhythm of a song of praise to the dead. The funeral of Full Bosom Jefferson next week will be worthy and successful as a well rehearsed drama.

On through the long blazing hours of the morning they pick, bodies growing limp with the heat and fingers sore with the picking. Sweat pours down backs and over chests, till the single dresses that are all most of the women wear stick to their forms, and outline great fat buttocks and flopping breasts and the bulging bellies of the pregnant pickers. But the awaited whistle of a distant train acts as a strengthener. When the train on the Y.D. railroad, the Yellow Dog, leaves Robinsonville, one of the "pups on the Yellow Dog" as they call their little Delta towns, it nears the time for dinner.

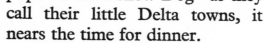

Over this sea of cotton comes a man on a stately white mule. Between the rows he passes; and mule and sunlit shirt and sacks thrown across the mule's back and cotton in the field, all these compete with one another in whiteness. It is as though we look upon a winter scene, and the garish colors of the dresses of the women pickers, and the more delicate pale yellows of the cotton blossoms, turning to pink, are butterflies that have confused the seasons and alight upon a snow-covered world.

And now sacks grow heavy and drag back the feet that tread the earth. The time of weighing is here; three sacks a day, each sack holding from seventy-five to ninety-five pounds, and fifty cents to be paid for one hundred pounds of cotton: this is the burden of the pickers' thoughts, as they bend and ache and pull their bodies across the unending field. Sacks are heaved across shoulders, and as the black tarpaulin-covered sides to the sacks lie against the clothing of the pickers, the torn white shirt, the frayed coat, the old stockings that cover the bare arms against the scratchings of the cotton, they sprinkle upon them in a black cloud of dust the earth of the cotton field. The abler pickers have gathered already around the cotton house and the steelyard. Like enormous white caterpillars, great filled sacks lie about on the ground, awaiting their turn to be weighed. The voices of pickers are loud in dispute as the colored man puts the iron hook through the drawstring, sliding the weight notch by notch down the scale. Lulu Brown shakes her fist in his face and her red-lacquered fingernails look cruel against the bloom on her black hands.

"There's full ninety pound in that sack if'n there's one pound," she yells. "Full ninety, I tells you."

But the serious Negro sitting in the shade before the house, in high rubber boots that give him a sense of remoteness from these mere pickers, enters the name Lulu Brown in his book, with the figure 78 irrevocably against it.

Into the cotton house are emptied the filled sacks, and there is nothing but the grey scrawl of a pencil in a book as evidence of the long hours of bending and picking of Sylvester Johnson and Love-Bird Jennings, Susie and her children and the frail old Negro woman in the crimson bandanna. The cotton lies in one great, impersonal heap within the pen.

Back to the picking troops the gang, back to the blazing heat of noon. Throughout the rest of the day, till the sun sinks red beyond the Mississippi, tingeing the cotton locks pink and throwing a warm bloom upon the hard black earth and the black skins of the pickers, throughout the day the thirty-nine colored people pick, and the man on the stately white mule collects the filled sacks. Like beasts of burden they tread the rows, and the sacks drag upon the ground behind them, with the weight of plow or harrow.

Dusk falls suddenly, and when the sun withdraws from the field the white of the unpicked cotton gives a chill look to the countryside, contradicting the heat that rises still from the earth. And as the pickers disperse for the night it is with the surety that tomorrow will bring the same hard heat to the earth they tread, and that the same blistering sun will blaze upon their bending backs.

Over the Delta country the gins are busy. Loaded wagons await their turn at the "telescope" that sucks the cotton up into the gin. Within the pale grey-green buildings, the tin buildings, the seed is blown separate from the cotton, and bales are put under high pressure in the compress, that they may take up less room. And the Negroes who alone know what it means to pick cotton, see with never failing distress that one thousand pounds of cotton is reduced in ginning to half its weight. The sickish scent of cottonseed oil

9

floats from the mills upon the hot air, and along the roads of the Mississippi Delta lie stray white locks of cotton, fallen from the loaded wagons. Cotton sticks to the sweating heads of the Negroes, till it is as though they had turned white-haired and white-browed; and as the mules that pull the wagons to the gin grow hot, the lint dapples their bodies and gives them the strangest white moustaches. It lies upon clothes and naked pickaninnies. It strays into cabin and plantation.

For cotton is over everything. It is master here, and man its servant. In the lobbies of the big hotels in Memphis, in Vicksburg, the plantation owners, the cotton sellers, the cotton factors meet and talk. And as they talk, it is against a background of ghosts—ghosts that haunt the Peabody in Memphis, ghosts that stepped off river steamers up the cobbled slope of the bank of the Mississippi in Vicksburg, ghosts who had opened balls in New Orleans and Natchez. They listen, these ghosts, for the calliopes of the great white side-wheelers, and spectre river steamers carry unsubstantial passengers within their overdecorated saloons, dancing and drinking and gambling. The old romantic life of the Deep South lives on, its artery the Mississippi. But it is no thing of flesh and blood. It is merely the indestructible existence of a world of phantoms. Upon the cotton fields reality endures, as aching feet tread the endless cotton rows, and tired bodies drag their sacks across the hard black earth. In an unsought moment of hypersensitivity, along the streets of Memphis, on the river front of New Orleans, the taste of this lost world of romance is upon the lips of one's spirit, and truth is obscured by cloying scent of magnolia, till cotton means the tinselled gaiety of the world of Lafayette or the soft pale cheek of a Natchez belle—soft and pale as the thick magnolia blossoms in the silvery moonlight. And then, as the spirit braces itself to honesty, the pale cheeks of the Natchez belle, the delicious gallantry of her escort, the white columns of the plantation house, all these withdraw before the stark power of truth. And, thinking of cotton, I see again "white gold" heaped upon the porch of a Negro shack, or "bumblebee" cotton against the red earth of North Carolina. I see a clump of pickers resting on the side of the main road near Bremen, Georgia, and the shadow of a telegraph pole throws a band of brilliant blue across the surface of the three great baskets of picked cotton. I hear the drone of the gang as it sings its way along relentlessly shadeless rows. I search for boll weevils and cotton worms, and with the pickers I share the fear of hurricanes in the lowlands of the Atlantic seaboard. I look upon gins and bales and bagging and ties, and watch colored babies playing among the cotton in the waiting wagons. All these I know, all these and the patient figures that chop cotton through the heat of the day. And, knowing these, I know too that I have seen the truth; for I have seen man in servitude to a growing plant.

WATER MILLS AND MILLERS

T WENT BACK to the days of early childhood, this magic surrounding water mills and millers. It ran through familiar nursery rhymes and brought a gasp of wonder to the city-bred child as she heard for the first time, in an English village, the growl of the wooden wheel. "There was a jolly miller and he lived by himself . . ." The child ran from her grandmother's side and stumbled in a puddle. Her coat was ochred with mud, but even the certainty of a beating could not destroy her excitement.

"As the wheel went round he . . ." The roar of the water drowned the remembrance now of all nursery rhymes, all childhood dances. At the corner of the lane the form of the mill appeared austere against lush water meadows, the severity of its outline softened by the curves of a blossoming pear tree. Into the swirl of water dropped the little white petals, blown down by the breeze. They dropped into the dark swirling waters and were swept round and round until they disappeared from sight in the white foam at the foot of the fall. The child stood by the millpond, and magic enfolded her.

"One hand in the hopper and the other in . . ." But where was the miller? She looked from the pond to the far end of the mill itself, past the water meadows that lay golden with kingcups, past the blossoming pear tree. And now, above the roar of the waters, she could hear other sounds: the crunch of wagon wheels upon a gravel road, the whine of an unoiled pulley, the low gruff murmur of men talking.

"Oh, Sandy he belongs to the mill,
And the mill belongs to Sandy still."

12

It was exactly like the picture in her new book of nursery rhymes.

In front of the mill stood a great red wagon, and down from the pulley at the top, just under the peak of the hipped roof, down came bulging sacks of flour. And the sacks were piled into the waiting wagon, and over everything—wagon and horses and men—lay a film of white. He was there, her miller. He leaned across the opened half-door, and flour greyed the shaggy hair of his eyebrows and lay thick in the deep wrinkles of his face.

"Come here." But Grandmother's voice was so far away that it seemed less loud than the hum of bees in the blossoming pear tree.

It was the darkness that beckoned to the child, the darkness inside the mill itself. She would slip in there, in at the opening of the lower part of the door, when the miller was turning the other way. She crouched by the heap of empty sacks upon a rejected millstone, tracing the blurred pattern of the harp with her fingers as she waited.

The whole place shook and trembled. She crept among the shadowed sacks, beneath vibrating beltings and aged beams, and the great building trembled and quivered. She listened, shaking in rhythm with the mill. Suddenly a thought came to her: Weren't there always rats and mice in a mill—rats and mice that gnawed at the tawny sacks? Thinking this, she grew scared and ran from the dark corner among the unground grain. She ran towards the light of the broken window panes, where the sun slanted through the flour-filmed air. The sun turned everything in its path to a deep, muted gold. It lighted upon the grain in the opened sacks. The child filled her hands with the golden grain, and it splattered upon the floor of the mill with a noise like a hail storm. Rats and mice and the distant call of a grandmother were forgotten. She was sowing bread.

Across the years I remember a water mill in Wiltshire. It was a very old one that dated from the time of the Domesday Book, and the miller with his twelve sons tried in vain to escape from the thraldom of their mill. It was a force too strong for them to cope with. Out to the cities would spread the twelve sons, out to far countries and new hemispheres. But the old mill would get them in the end, and like spellbound creatures they would drift back—back to the damp wooden building with the slippery steps and the sound of the race, back to the musty darkness within and the throbbing that was like the strong pulse of a living heart. The heartbeats of the mill were felt in the hills of India, on the sheep plains of Australia, and its sons were powerless to resist.

And then there was the desolate mill in Dorset, with the miller's little lunatic son who spent entire mornings braiding and unbraiding my hair and tying it in gay-colored ribbons. Playing by the race, we would sing songs to each other, we two children, and the miller would leave his work and come and sit with us and stroke our heads with his floury hands. There was a gentleness about him, and a softness, as though he understood and loved all life. Thinking back upon him now, after many years, it seems to me that all millers have this same gentleness. It is as if they feel themselves to be the feeders of mankind.

But it is about America that I am supposed to be writing, and all these mills of my early life were in England, scattered over the countryside among the purple fritillary fields of Berkshire or in the bleakness of Hardy's Wessex. Here in America, I told myself, over here in this new country you will miss your water mills.

There is one unfailing softener of nostalgia, and that is the universality of the things of the earth. Transplanted to America, I sought barns and harvests, that I might with more ease put roots down. It was in seeking these that I found water mills.

The first one was in the mountains of North Carolina. I remember the evening in September that I discovered it, a golden evening with the countryside misty in asters. The mill was so incorporated into the rocks on the side of a hill, beneath the main road, that I did not see it as I passed. It was the stumbling, growling sound of the turning of the wheel that made me stop and search. Following the sound, I went down a stony rough path at the side of the road, winding my way around great clumps of goldenrod and flowering asters. A snake slid among the grasses; my legs were torn by thorns. It was hardly the well trodden path to a prosperous mill, I felt, as I disentangled myself from protesting undergrowth. But below me I saw a more worn path that led across the tiny cove to a cabin on the opposite hillside. It must be there that the miller trod each day. Seeing that worn path, I felt hopeful of finding the mill still running.

But of course I should find the mill still running. For one moment I had forgotten the stumbling, growling sound of the water wheel. And now, as I freed myself from the tangle of undergrowth, I

15

saw the wheel. Green slime and lichen covered it in patches and caught the sunlight that sparkled on the dripping water. The wheel turned with a rumble and then stopped, and as it stopped the sparkling water tumbled over the sluices, high up against the roof. Again the wheel turned, and as it crept into the shadow below it was hidden beneath a blaze of sunlit goldenrod.

A pear tree with two great trunks burst its way through the roof of the mill. Or was the mill built around the tree? But no, the pear was not of that age. The mill was so primitive that I felt no surprise at the way tree and roof merged: wood of tree and wood of shingle roof, it was right that they should be barely distinguishable, one from the other. Suddenly, looking at it, I saw the blossoming pear tree against the water mill of my earliest childhood, and I felt at home. So, always, it seemed, should there be a leaning fruit tree against a mill.

Down more rocks I jumped, and I could see now right into the mill. The building was tottering with age, and I almost expected it to fall apart before me, shaken so violently as it was by each turn of the wooden wheel, which was as big as the mill itself.

There was a dark shape within, moving against the dark.

"Oh, Sandy he belongs to the mill,
And the mill belongs to Sandy still."

The old miller was a hairy creature, like a blond walrus, with a long wavy moustache and locks of fair hair that tumbled about his head. He had the height of a mountain man and, noticing the way he was forced to bend his head as he moved, I wondered why the mill had not been built higher; for this mountain country was a land of giants. He sat upon rocks as he rested, and the inner wall of his gristmill was the rough rock itself. Only the splintering, rotting boards and the crumbling shakes of the roof separated him from the mountain side, and sheltered him from heat of sun or drenching of rain. As my eyes grew used to the darkness, I looked more closely at the miller. He was so sad-faced that I felt there must have been tragedy in his life. He was silent, and when he did speak at all, in answer to my questionings, it was in a voice so husky that it seemed as though his throat were covered with the dust of his own ground corn meal.

The mill went on grinding, and I sat beside him, and no words passed between us. But the silence was not of antagonism. It was the silence of a man who has lived alone so long that he has grown beyond the need for speech. Here between the folds of the mountains, what use were the formed words of human man? It was the language of the rocks that the miller understood, the song of his stream, the changing pattern of shadows upon his hillsides. Sitting silently beside him there, in the darkness of the tiny mill, I became aware of a gentle kindness in him, and a deep wisdom.

It is strange how much one can learn of another human creature without the help of words, and when the sun sank low enough to slant into the cracks of the wooden boards at the side of the mill, and the miller raised himself from the rocks and heaved a sack of corn meal across his shoulder, to leave for home, I had begun to understand that there is even something limiting about verbal language. Things more strong than words told this man's tale, things like the extravagant curving of the worn path he took each night, that proclaimed his gentleness towards bushes and little trees; so, I knew, he could never destroy an obstructing plant, but would wind his way around it. And so, as I watched his face, I knew, too, that he had within him no bitterness about tragedy. And I knew as strongly that it was unworthy of him and of me that I should even question within myself the particular nature of this tragedy. Sitting silently with him in his mill, I had begun to absorb the dignity of these mountains. This miller's life was in tune with the mythology of earth and ran strong with the pattern of the inevitable suffering in nature. Pain

17

to this man was nothing against which to feel resentment; for the storm-struck tree stands scarred and blasted and does not complain: it has budded and blossomed and has felt the rising of sap and the

swelling of fruit. This man of silence, with the bent shoulders and the limp to his walk, had bridged the division between human and tree and earth, and no more should one ask of him that he talk in words than that the sourwood tree or the sweet gum should explain the curve to this bough or the twist to that trunk. The wind and the rain and the sun had formed trees and rocks and miller and any difference among them was untrue. The corn grew in the upright fields upon the mountain sides; it sprouted and tasselled and swelled and was shucked, and this man was but the instrument that attended the water-grinding of the corn and let it run slowly through the rocks, of the same fabric as the sun that drew the corn shoots above the earth or the rain that swelled the ears. Silently he heaved the sack of corn meal across his shoulder and limped to the open door of the mill, leaving me to follow.

Among the clumps of goldenrod we wound our way, and a great bush of "hearts bustin' with love" bent its crimson and orange fruit towards us. He leaned from it, that he might not brush it with his sack, and I knew I had been right when I had felt him to be of the substance of tree and earth.

As the path turned to cross the little creek at the base of the cove, our ways divided. He limped with care over the wooden footbridge and I could see that the worn path curved among rocks and undergrowth to a cabin on the hillside, as broken-down as the mill itself. But warmth came from that cabin, as from a bird's nest in the crook of a tree or the entrance to a rabbit burrow among ferns. My miller was going to earth.

I turned to look back as I went my own way to the highroad, and the lengthening shadow of the man by now had touched the doorstep of his cabin, drawing him home.

But not all the millers in the mountains of North Carolina were so silent. I remember a miniature overshot water mill that had been in use for more than seventy-five years. The shingle roof was rough and the flume was falling almost to pieces; but the wooden wheel still turned. The race ran round in a large circle, and a bank had been built to support the flume. The whole place had the appearance of a toy and, coming upon it unexpectedly round a bend of a dirt road, I felt as though I had been transported to the world of Grimm. I looked for a fairy-tale miller and his people. And perhaps I was not far wrong, for treading softly upon the grass I was the unintentional eavesdropper to a love scene. It was the miller himself, making love to a mountain girl. The picture belonged to the days of Herrick.

The miller lay upon the grass, and his arm was around the mountain girl. Her hair tumbled upon her shoulders, and his hand lifted it and stroked it as he sang.

For he was singing to her. He was singing a ballad that his forebears had brought with them as an imperishable belonging from across the sea. And suddenly it seemed to me as though a tuck had been taken in time and the life of my own forebears flowed without interruption into this life here, in the Carolina mountains. Gratefully, I knew I belonged.

But the miller was wooing her now, and he was wooing her in

words of such beauty that they did not seem to belong to these days:

"Come with me, my true love sweetheart. Come with me and I will give you joy . . ."

Ashamed to be listening, I crept away. But magic surrounded the dilapidated mill with its aged flume and the waiting wheel.

I think the saddest mill I ever found was a deserted one. We had driven for many miles, with sacks of corn to be water-ground—not steam-ground with the burnt taste of the heat, but water-ground with slowness and care—and leaving the car at the far end of a covered bridge, had toted our sacks along the nearly hidden path through the edge of the woods.

We did not like the look of the ground around us. There were no marks of footprints in the damp clay, no wagon ruts. Briers wove a crisscross pattern before us, and honeysuckle crept into the middle of the path. Surely we were not mistaken. Surely, the last time we had come here, there had been signs of footsteps and the marks of horses' hooves.

It was not the fact that the footpath was rough and overgrown that distressed us, for always, it seemed to me, water mills lay hidden at the end of deserted lanes. I had wandered down many such lanes in my search, and knew by now that never did one find a gristmill near to a highroad. "Is Bush's Mill along this way?" we had asked once of a farmer on a rough dirt road. The farmer's face had glowed as he directed us. "Why," he smiled, "that's where I got my last wife. And you go back to the main road, and take the fifth turning to the right and along that dirt road till you get to a great sycamore tree. Then you bear to the right again, and past two or three tumble-down cabins for a piece until you reach yet another turning, this time to the left. Go along that dirt road until you see a small gravel pit and some cutover land. There you keep straight on, neither to right nor left, down the narrow dirt road through the woods until you come to the mill." And we had found that mill, on a drenching day with the lane sticky in red Carolina clay, and the car skidding like a mad thing; we had sought it as a child seeks an egg in an Easter egg hunt, and when we had found it the mill was as complete and miniature as a toy itself. Rain pitted the surface of the millpond and shone upon the piles of corncobs dumped in the bed of the stream. It was a complete picture of a water mill.

But this path we trod now, this worried us. Our sacks grew heavier and heavier, the farther along the lane we went. Could it possibly be that the mill had fallen to pieces at last? It was running, a year ago, even though it had been tumbling so to ruin that it hardly stood upright. We did not give up hope until we turned the last bend in the lane. And then we understood. Without saying a word to each other, we lowered our sacks of corn to the ground. They would not be needed.

But the silence of the water wheel stood out against another silence. There was no sound of the trickling of water. The river had dried up in this last season's drought.

We went into the mill. There, as I remembered, was the small seat at the entrance, worn smooth over a century. And looking upon this smooth seat, I thought of the countless men who had sat upon it, while they waited for their corn to be ground. Slowly the corn would have been ground, slowly and without heat, and slowly, too, would they have talked, these country men, bringing to the miller in his solitude the gossip of the neighborhood, and the philosophy of their isolated lives. And as I thought of all that had been talked of, from this smoothly worn seat, I was overcome with the pity of it that such wisdom and knowledge had been lost to us. I could think of the wars that had been discussed, the harvests, the hurricanes, the sicknesses. And always, I could imagine, the miller quietly would have listened and pondered before he answered, slow and weighty as one who lives alone.

I turned from the seat, and the air quivered with the wings of dirt

21

daubers, nesting in all the corners of the old mill. There, still, was the millstone, and there the dipper, and the box and the drums, and there, too, were the great wooden pegs that secured one rafter to another. Nothing yet had been pillaged. The floors gaped with holes, and the rafters and beams crumbled and sagged. I walked up the small wood staircase, and it creaked and shifted with each step I took. Soon, I knew, colored folks would come and take away this timber for firewood, and nothing would be left but the millstone, which before long would be hidden beneath the trails of honeysuckle. And I felt very sad, for I knew that here was the death of a craft—the old craft of water grinding, a craft so completely satisfying because, like that of the potter, it is bound up with the true needs of man and goes back to the beginning of time.

On the dry rocky bed of the river lay a heap of corncobs, waiting to be carried downstream in the current when the mill was working. But they would have to wait for the years to reduce them to dust; the mill would never work again. Above the slope stands a brick and mortar chimney, marking the site of the house which had belonged to the great-grandfather of the miller. They will stand here, crumbling chimney and derelict millstone, memorials to a family of millers. And when unborn children dance and sing to the tune of "The Jolly Miller," it will be about something that they do not understand. For the water mill will have ceased to exist.

HOW THE DEVIL CAME
TO THE REVEREND HILL

WHICH of you isn't willin' to lend the Lord God a nickel or a dime, and He give the whole world to you?"

A strange dark cry cut across the auctioneer's chant. I looked towards the far aisles of the tobacco market, bewildered by the wording of the cry.

"God will bless a cheerful giver. Yes, I say unto you, God will bless him a hundredfold."

What did this mean? Who was giving? Here in this market of prancing auctioneers, here beneath this gurgling song of tobacco prices, was it possible that here something actually was being given?

But no. There before me I saw the auctioneer; hot and fat, he sprang from foot to foot as he crooned the chant of the tobacco market. I watched his face as the bubbled words came from his coarse mouth. Here was no sign of giving. Here was no thought for the Lord God. Necktie askew, straw hat tumbled to the back of his head, he looked as ungenerous as anyone I had ever seen. I watched him more closely as he vibrated to the excitement of his own chant. No: emphatically here was no cheerful giver.

What, then, did it all mean? Who was it who uttered this cry?

Wondering, I looked farther still into the distant corners of this great market. I discovered nothing. About me rushed the crowds of buyers and sellers, Negro porters and excited peddlers. From the mouths of none of these came this dark call.

I listened yet more carefully. It came from my left, this song. It came from beyond the rectangle of light that was the entrance to the market. I moved towards it now as it lifted its force again in a beseeching cry.

"Nobody can stop me talkin' 'bout Jesus. No, nobody on this earth of the Lord's can stop me talkin' 'bout the Lord Jesus . . ."

It's a Negro, I told myself. No one but a Negro could put such intensity into simple words.

I followed the cry till I found myself on the sidewalk beyond the entrance to the market. The sun blazed upon me. My feet crushed peanut shells. My nostrils were filled with the sickly scent of tobacco. I passed rows of aged Negroes sitting in the sun upon the cement ledge of the great building. I stumbled against trucks laden with tobacco. But I scarcely remarked anything about me. Spellbound, I followed this cry.

And then I saw the singer. He sat alone at the far end of the cement ledge. His face was lifted to the skies; his eyes were closed. The sun shone upon the grease of his coat and glistened on the moisture of his hot face. He seemed to me to be one of the oldest Negroes I had ever seen, and the curling wisps of hair that fell beneath his worn felt hat were misty grey.

"When the po' blind man lost his eyesight he lost his best friend. Yes, I tell you, he lost his best friend."

And so that's it, I realized. He's a blind beggar.

Walking softly, I went near to him. The lids flickered and opened, disclosing two film-coated eyeballs. The sightless eyes faced the fierce glare of the sun. I tried to sit beside him without making a sound, but with the sharpened ears of the blind he had heard me, and already he had turned to me.

"Yes, I say unto you, the Lord loves them what gives—the Lord that give the whole world to us; yes, I say, the earth and the sky and the little bright stars at night. He give us the sun by day and the dew at evenfall. He sent us the flowers and the birds, the rainbows and the sunsets. And He give us eyes that we might behold His

24

glories. Repent ye, I tell you, repent ye that the Lord God may not take your eyes from you. Repent that ye be not blinded."

I looked at the glistening face beside me, with its unseeing eyes that remembered rainbows and sunsets, earth and sky and the little bright stars. I gazed into the tired old face that glowed with faith, and I knew that I sat with a man of vision.

"The Lord God, there is one sin that He never forgives; and that is the sin of a man thinkin' he be better than his brethren. Yes, I say unto you, the Lord makes a man pay when he is prideful."

The people jostled one another on the sidewalk; raspingly the tobacco-laden trucks changed gear. But the old blind Negro beggar was unconfused by these sounds, even as his filmed eyeballs faced the sun without flinching.

He burst then into song. "Somebody's knockin' at your door . . ." he chanted, and, turning towards me, he seemed to be pleading with me alone. I listened, and the low dark voice drowned the roar of the tobacco market and the clang of the traffic.

"Tell me about yourself," I asked him as he finished his singing. "Tell me how you got this faith. Tell me how you conquered your blindness, so that it is as though you had true vision."

He shifted his white-painted stick to the far hand and settled back on the ledge against the brick wall, as though to tell a long tale. I could feel he was glad of an audience.

"It's a lesson from the Lord God, it is," he began. "It's a lesson to show that no man livin' has the right to think hisself better than his brethren. Hit's a lesson that the Lord Jesus done give to me that I mought be laid low."

The aged mouth seemed to quiver at its corners, and the unseeing eyes blinked.

"I was a preacher once," he went on. "I was a preacher in a Baptist church way out in the foothills of Virginia. I was a preacher in that church for thirty years, I was, and there weren't no soul in that church, no nor in any church around, that I didn't know if'n he'd sinned or not. I watched the courtin's and the weddin's, and when my ol' Aunt Sallie was called in at a bornin' I could'a' told her nine months befo' that she'd sho be wanted jest then. But my 'tracted meetin's got smaller and smaller each year as August come around, and my mourners' bench it weren't no longer filled with rows of bowed heads, for there weren't no mo' sinners to save, and I had to wait for the little uns to get borned, so they mought be caught in sin and baptized."

A colored passer-by stopped before us. He placed a dime in the open hand of the beggar.

"The Lord will bless you for this gift," said the old Negro. "He sho' will bless you a hundredfold."

Fumblingly he put the coin in his vest pocket as he turned again my way.

"My woman, she will be glad of this," he went on. "She brings me here each day at eight and she fotches me way home at four. And never one day do she forget to come for the ol' nigger beggar; and I gives her my takin's, be they small or big. The Lord God Almighty, He been good to me with my womenfolks. When the Devil chased me from my church, my old woman she found out where I was gone and she followed me, like the good Christian she were. But when the Lord He strikes me blind—it were one mornin' as I waked and pulled out my watch to look at the time and I finds that I be blind and can't see no time at all—when He strikes me blind I turns to my wife and my crippled boy. 'Wife and son,' I says, 'this is the Lord's doin' and blessed be the name of the Lord.' Then befo' many days is past she gets up and leaves me and takes the crippled boy with her and I am left lonesome. Why then, in the meanwhile time the good Lord He never forgets the old blind beggar, for one mornin' another woman comes into my life—a sanctified woman, she were, and given over to the ways of the Lord—and she

26

stops and talks to me and asks me if it be true I'd been a preacher
and would I like for her to take me to a prayer meetin'. Yes, I tells
you, the Lord were good to me, for that sanctified woman she lived

with me for five years, and she were soft and gentle, even though I
could see her only with my hands."

He stroked the greasy cloth of his knee, as though it were the soft
dark skin of the Negro woman.

"But one day this woman, this sanctified woman, she comes over quare, and she says she has been sinnin', and she goes. And once again I am left lonesome, till once again the good Lord He sends me this woman now, that comes and fotches me at four each evenin'."

A great truck of tobacco had stopped in the road before us, its motor roaring. The old beggar paused in his story, and I was afraid that I should hear no more. I sat quietly by his side as he sang "Rock my soul in the bosom of Abraham." But then he was silent.

I think he had forgotten that I was sitting there, and I would have moved quietly away if I had not been puzzled by one short sentence in his story. "When the Devil chased me from my church," he had said. I wanted to hear more about this.

"But the Devil," I began. "You said the Devil chased you from your church. How did it happen?"

"Most everybody knows that hereabouts," he said. "Most everybody can tell you how the Devil come to the Reverend Hill. Why, the li'l boys will come and ask me: 'Uncle Tom,' they'll say, 'Uncle Tom, won't you tell us again how you was chased by the Devil, and him all black, with horns and fire comin' out from his mouth?'"

A scared look came into the face. Terror seemed to run even into the sightless eyes. The hands grasped nervously, one the white-painted stick, the other the greasy cloth knee. It was almost as though the actual body had shrunk from fear.

"It was like this," he began. "It was a lesson from the Lord. I'd been preachin' in Pleasant Grove for thirty years, and it seemed to me that I was a mighty man of God, and that my folks there in the church befo' me, sittin' in the seats, was all so weak in faith that I was scared for them in the Judgment Day. And so each Sunday as I preaches I ends my sermon in the same way—for thirty years I ended it like that. I always said to my folks there: 'All you people here, yo' prayers don't have no effect, because yo' faith is too weak, yo' religion is no good. Now why don't you be like me? If the Devil was to come into this church at this moment you would all be so

weak you would run away from him, and you would leave Ol'
Uncle Tom to face the Devil alone. Why don't you have the faith
of Ol' Tom?' And I hollered at them folks so as to put faith into them,
and they trembled in their seats with fear."

The old man shook his head from side to side, with a little moan.

"But one day the Lord God He comes to test me out. And I
fails Him. Yessir, I fails the Lord God Almighty. It was an evenin'
in July, and the whipperwill had started a-whirlin' in the valleys,
comin' sometimes so close to the church that it seemed almost to
drown my preachin'. I was jest sayin' 'you would leave Ol' Tom to
face the Devil alone' when what do I see there, at the far end of the
church, but the Devil hisself. He was there as big as life, all black and
hairy, with great claws standin' out from his arms and mighty horns
straight out from the top of his head; and from his mouth, jest like
it is said in the Scriptures, out from his mouth come spouts of
flamin' fire. I stood there still as a pillar, and the people must have
wondered what had happened to me. I stood there, and I sho must
have had terror in my face, for first thing I knows I hears a rustle in
the seats and all heads is turned back to the end of the church. And
they must have seen the Devil, too, for they rushes from their seats
and screams and runs down to the church door, to get away. But
that Devil, he never concerns hisself with my folks there. It's Ol'
Uncle Tom what he's after, jest to prove me out with the Lord God.
And I fails the Lord God. Yessir, I fails Him badly. I stands there
starin' at the Devil, but it's with fear in my heart and terror in my
bones. Like as it was a dream, I sees the Devil brushin' aside Lulu
Thompson and Ready Smiles, Eulalie Washin'ton and old Aunt
Sophy. I sees him brushin' them aside jest like they wasn't there.
I suppose they all runs from the church, but all I sees is the Devil
makin' straight for Ol' Tom. The fire from his mouth is hot enough
that I feels it upon my face. And suddenly I runs. I leaps the chairs
to the right and runs across to the wall at the right of the church; but

the Devil he follows me there. I runs round befo' him to the left side of the church, but the Devil he done follow me again, till I feels that fire comin' from his nostrils and his mouth like unto a flamin' sword. 'Lord A'mighty, save me!' I cried. 'Lord A'mighty, save a miserable sinner. Lord God of Hosts, I's a deep-dyed sinner what wants to come to mercy.' But then I feels the great claws scrapin' down my back, and I screams again to the Lord for help. 'Save me, save me,' I shouts . . ."

The old blind beggar was reliving his terror so truly that he had raised his voice to a scream, and a small crowd of passers-by had gathered around us, listening to his tale. All unseeing, he continued.

"And the Devil, he do seem to leap most on me. And I runs from the left side of the church, where I had begun to sidle against the wall, and I runs and I runs and I runs—and never did it seem to me that my church was so powerful long. I runs to the door that stood so far away and so small, there like a square of dim light in the darkness. I runs to the door and out of that church I runs, with the Devil after me. I 'spects my folks seen me run, but I never knowed. All I could think of was that great black hairy Devil runnin' after me, his horns ready to lift me up and carry me off to Hell. All I could feel was the heat of that fire from his flamin' mouth, and the swish of his long black tail. I runs down the street, past the schoolhouse and the store. I runs along by the edge of Mr. John Elliot's cornfield, thinkin' like I could run and hide in there. But the Devil he runs so fast that he is almost on me and I feels those great sharp claws scrapin' me down my back. 'Lord God A'mighty,' I cries again—and surely, I thinks, surely the Lord God can hear them cries, Him what watches the littlest sparrow—'Lord God of Mercy, save me. Save me, and Ol' Tom he won't never think again as how he is better than others. Save me, and I won't never be prideful no more.' But the Devil's claws is in my back, and I can feel that each claw is makin' a burn in my body. So I runs still further, till I comes to the pine wood."

A sigh shook the old body beside me, a sigh so violent that even his knees trembled.

"Yes," I said, "and what then? Did you escape him among the pines?"

"I runs into the pines," he went on. "I runs there, with the Devil screamin' now into my ears. And seein' that I knows each tree by shape I dodges around them, thinkin' to trick him. But it do seem that the old Devil he done know those pine trees by heart, too, as well as the Reverend Hill, fo' he do trick me mo' than I do trick him. And there I am, in the deepenin' dusk, with the fire from his mouth flamin' brighter and brighter, till it is like the gates of Hell itself. . . . And then—and then—somehow I hardly knows exactly what did happen then. It seems as if the Devil gets his horns all caught in some tree, for he reels and falls on me, horns and all, and we gets tangled up in one another. And the next thing I knows it is nearly dawn, and I wakes stiff and scared. But there weren't no Devil to be seen, and I were so stunned I mought almost have thought I'd dreamt it all if it weren't that there, on the

ground by my side, was tufts of black hair I'd tore from the Devil, and two horns—looking for all the world like the horns from Mr. John Elliot's old cow that he'd had to slaughter a few days befo'. The Lord God must have sont me mighty powerful strength to wrench them horns from the Devil in my fright. And there, as I looked around, there stood the same pine trees that I had always knowed."

"And then?" I asked. "What happened then?"

The old Negro shook his head.

"Why, then it all comes upon me. It's a lesson from the Lord God, I tells myself. And I gets up to walk away. I gets up to leave my church, for I knows that the Lord God means it. I knows right then that I never can face my people again. I knows that I has betrayed them to the Devil. So I gets up and I walks and I walks and I walks. And I 'spects I walks somehow from Virginia to North Carolina."

He stopped, and as he sat there, silent and unmoving, I knew that the old stumbling feet were retracing the endless straight roads of North Carolina, which seem to lead into the sky itself.

"And then there was long years," he moaned. "They was lean years and they was lonesome years, even though my wife and child did follow me and live with me awhile, and they was years of repentin' for Ol' Tom, they was. But the Reverend Hill he learnt his lesson, and he never preached a sermon again. And lest he should forget the lesson that the Lord God sent him, the Lord set His sign upon him, and did take my eyes from me."

Four o'clock struck from a church at the end of the street. It was like the fit ending to a tale. And as the last stroke sounded above the roar of the traffic and the bustle of the tobacco market, I saw the little figure of a colored woman wind her way towards us among the crowds upon the sidewalk. Dressed in shabby, shiny black, her white kid shoes seemed to balance the white of the old man's stick. Gently she leaned over him as she reached us, and taking him by the arm, led him from me without a word. Where he had sat beside me I saw an empty space. The blind Negro preacher beggar had gone from me forever.

CORN SHUCKING

IETER BREUGHEL would have loved it, I felt, as I saw all those flat round potato pies. I knew just the picture he would have painted, with the dark orange circles covering tables and bureaus, like huge checkers on a board. And it wouldn't have made much difference that the figures were Negroes, for there was the same jollity about these colored people that we find in Breughel's own laughing Flemish peasants.

I count the round orange-colored pies: eighteen of them, and more still to come, so Sugarine tells me.

"But you jest come along with me and I'll show you what else we've got," she winks.

Bureau drawers are opened, and ghostlike coverings of white cheesecloth removed, disclosing four enormous iced layer cakes. Side tables and cupboards everywhere are covered with caldrons of stewed sweet potato mash, and on the cooking stove stand pans of chicken and onions, and beef for hash. A warm smell lies over everything, and there is a sense of excitement in the air. A very old Negro woman in a pale magenta print stands at the table, cutting out thin shapes of dough for dumplings to go with the chicken. Everyone is busy.

Three days now have gone to the preparing of the feast, three days devoted with ritualistic care to mixing and cooking and baking. But so much is there still to be done that the shucking, planned for today, has had to be put off until tomorrow.

A tiny colored boy comes in at the open door and sidles up to the aged woman.

"Grandmammy," he says, "I've smeared my rabbit gums with

33

apple juice on the outside of the trap, and I've speared apple cores inside the trap, and yet it don't seem as if no rabbits 'll get ketched in time for the shuckin'."

The old woman in the pale magenta print pats the boy's head with a floury hand.

"Don't you mind, honey baby," she comforts him. "The Lord God will send them rabbits into your trap if'n He thinks as you should have them. Now run along and leave me alone, else we won't be havin' the shuckin' tomorrow after all."

The small colored child runs off, the white imprint of a hand upon his black head, like a blessing from the Lord God.

I never saw so many people in this kitchen before. Sugarine Burney's sisters and cousins have come over to help her with the preparing of the feast. And neighbors, too, are here, reaching up to the top shelves of cupboards to bring down pickled peaches, pickled cucumbers, pickled watermelon. Someone has brought out Sugarine's jars of preserved wild cherries, by mistake, and Sugarine Burney shrieks to her to put them back where she found them; tiny dark purple things, they are ready for her next spring, as a medicine against colds. The shrieks turn to laughter which ripples out and out, like circles in a pond, till the whole house is in an uproar of delight.

"Lordy, Lordy," shouts the grey-haired grandmother, "to think if'n we'd give' them wild cherries to the folks to eat like pickles, and my Sugarine cherishing them jest as if'n they was made of gold!" Her laughs shake the great fat body, and the hand that cuts the dough wobbles, till the dumplings are of the wildest shapes.

They are all so happy. They are happy in the ritualism of the corn-shucking feast. And looking at them here, these dusky women in their gay-colored prints, I know I watch the magic of harvest. This is a harvest festival, and it carries with it the triumphant joy of all harvests. In the great dark barns of England, my own people had sung and danced to the "Harvest Home," growing joyous and ir-responsible in the light of the harvest moon. So, too, did the sun-tanned peasants of the Mediterranean sing and dance and love and grow drunk with joy at the time of the harvesting of the grapes. I can see again the kitchen in the farmhouse at Saint-Clair, with the old woman making *rémoulade* and the host of neighbors helping with the cooking for the *vendange* dinner. And as I think back upon it, and then to these colored women here, it seems to me that one of the strongest things in the whole world is the sense of earth ritual. It overrides race and country and links everyone in a chain of rejoicing. I forget whether I am listening to the crooning drawl of the Carolina Negro or to the Latin tones of the Provençal peasant. The only thing that is of value is that man celebrates his harvest of the earth. And just as there was the division of the sexes at the time of the grape harvesting in the Mediterranean, or the day of hog killing in Mary-land, so that the men worked outside and the women tended the food within the house, so, here, it is the women who fill the kitchen and prepare the feast, while the men remain without, heaping the unshucked corn into the centre of the farmyard, where it sprawls like a wan limp stranded whale.

The color of the unshucked corn is the pale gold of winter sunlight. It is a scene of grey and gold, as the corn lies in the centre of the little farmyard, backed by unpainted wooden crib and gabled barn. It is a beautiful farmyard, enclosed by an old rail fence that separates it from the grove of dark cedars beyond, and the grey rocky ground where the rabbits live. The old rail fence is like a pair of great arms around the harvest of the year, and suddenly I think of sheepfolds I have known, where the sheep with their lambs are sheltered from the marauders without; and, thinking thus of sheepfolds, I know why there is a sense of safety within a farmyard. This enclosed yard holds within the hollow of its hands the sum of the year's harvest. Here, before me, as rustling, shaggy ears of corn, lies the ultimate

35

fruit of the spring rains that softened the earth and drew the shoots up to the light, of the wind that shook the flowers of the corn till they dropped their pollen upon the unformed ear, of the fierce sun of the North Carolina summer that ripened the swelled corn—all these forces have culminated in this sprawling mass within the old rail fence. Scent of the corn in flower, rustle of the great leaves in the wind, floss of tassels—here is their distillation.

The small colored boy pauses as he runs across the farmyard to the rabbit gums among the cedars, and as he looks at this mass it is with a certain triumph; he sees himself a few months back, searching for a younger sister who had got lost in the field of corn at the back of the smokehouse. Her cries had reached them, faint and distressed, from somewhere in that great forest of cornstalks that grew high above his head, higher even than his pappy's head. He lives again his own terror as his mammy had sent him out into the middle of that cornfield to look for the child. Nobody would ever know how scared he had been. And now that corn has been stripped, and lies here, ragged and powerless and untidy, while he goes on growing till he'll soon be as big as the tallest corn that ever grew. He walks to the cedar grove with triumph in his step.

Quietness creeps over the farmyard as winter evening falls, and only within the house is there commotion still. Into the night there will be voices in the kitchen, and the smell of warm cooked pies. But without, everything waits for tomorrow.

Tomorrow comes, but long before dawn Old Silas has wakened to the beat of rain upon his cabin roof. Humble before the tricks of Nature, he turns upon his bed to sleep once more. There will be no shucking today. Sugarine is wakened, too, by this sound of rain; but she is younger than Old Silas and less philosophical, and lying beside her man she thinks with anger of her cooking.

"Never one drop of rain for the last three weeks," she grumbles, "and now hit has to come today, to spoil everything."

She gets from the bed and looks out at the window. The dawn is hazy still and there is no break to be seen in the sky.

Over the countryside the colored people awaken to this sound of rain. But the great God-A'mighty is kind. By the time smoke rises from cabin chimneys and the scent of coffee is in the air and the grits have been cooked, the grey sky has formed itself into clouds, and a faint winter sun breaks through. And as this sun strikes upon little windows of negro cabins, upon the bucket by the well, the clapper of the dinner bell, the people hurry their steps, and from sheds and outhouses come the roar of motors and the grind of brakes. Old Silas goes to the stable to mount his mule, and the womenfolk at the farm throw more wood into the fire, that the chicken stew may cook.

And now through the sweet, rain-cleaned air, over the crimson clay of the North Carolina lanes, richened in color by the wet till there is almost a lilac bloom upon the earth, over the little rutty lanes roar and snort an assortment of old cars. They bump over hummocks and splash into puddles. They slither in the wet clay, and it is as though they would fall apart; but always they converge to Sugarine's farm. The buzzard, were he sentient, floating in the pale gold sky, would see many black specks, as it were on the spokes of a great wheel, moving to the central hub.

Old Silas trots along on his mule, as he has trotted for sixty-five corn shuckings. Ritual is strong within him today, strong enough to make him forget the pain that stabs his heart each time he moves a little faster. He looks around him at the quiet fields, where the ghosts of the year's harvests stand sentinel; shaded tones of brown and buff they stand, dead tobacco, dead cotton, dead corn. As the mule trots along he plants corn once again, and worms tobacco and chops cotton. He relives the tiredness of his body at the end of the day of cotton picking, and slumps on the mule as his legs give way and he creeps along the burning cotton field upon his knees.

39

But he has reached the farm, and the shouts of the gathering people recall him from his wanderings. There, under the acid yellow-green of the chinaberry trees, they gather and laugh, while out in the farmyard sprawls the stranded whale of corn, waiting to be shucked.

There is order in this rioting. As though in obedience to an unstated command, the people troop to the farmyard, carrying with them kitchen chairs that look strangely puny and lonesome out here in the yard. And today the men are joined by the women. Old Aunt Madge, in her white calico coat and a bandanna tied tight under a man's felt hat, laughs as she takes her place at the far end of the wooden bench by the corncrib. Silas already sits on the chair placed for him nearest the end of the pile, placed there that he may not have to throw the corn far when he shucks it. Around this great pile, in the curve of a semicircle, sit and stand the shuckers, on benches and chairs and upturned tin baths and baskets covered with sacks. The rain has been kind, for it has softened the corn; it will be less rough to the dark hands that wrench and tear the ears from the shucks—those shucks that look like the feathers of strange pale birds, ruffled in a fight. This same rain has darkened the earth around the pile, throwing a soft glow upon it that was lacking the day before when the earth was parched. And over the entire scene the grey weather—for the sun is hidden once again behind the blurred clouds—gives added brilliance to the colors of the shuckers, till the yellow of the label on the back of the suspenders of Uncle Silas's overalls shouts to the eye, and the blue jeans of the men and the bright clothes of the women are rich against the wan color of the dampened corn.

The first ear of corn spins through the air, across the piled heap; others rain down, and they lie upon the ground like a pale spreading pool. On and on, through the hours, the dark hands pull down the shucks, wrenching and twisting the ear from its covering, with a little turn of the wrist, so gently and with such skill that it is too deft for the onlooker to understand; hands get rough and sore with the shucking, and arms grow tired with the throwing of the ears across that great pile of corn. The pale little pool of ears mounts higher and higher, and the sound changes now from a dull thud at first, when ear struck wet ground, like muted raindrops, to a more pointed and brittle sound as ear falls upon ear. But still, all through, it is like the sound of heavy rain. Dried silk tassels stick to some of the ears, and are whirled off as the corn shoots through the air.

It is a duet of sound, this shucking: thud of falling ear, murmur and soft laughter of negro voices. The sounds weave into each other, and are of the fibre of earth. Sometimes a woman's laugh is raised above the murmuring level of this duet, as she teases the man by her side, or tries to disentangle her hand from his grip among the mottled unshucked ears. Sometimes the roar of a car breaks into the pattern as it brings to the gathering a belated helper.

But throughout the long morning the shucking goes on, and the great central mass of corn changes in shape and size and the piles of ears spread, till small pale pool joins with small pale pool in one big heap. The shuckers no longer sit on the solid earth of a farmyard. They seem now to float in a wild sea of shucks, a sea pale with rough foam. They float in the shape of a semicircle, and, as they bend forward to seize the ear from the pile, it is as if they were tossed by the waves. A young man gathers the shucks together, swaying from side to side as he plunges into this sea, hidden beneath it at times so that nothing of him is visible and he might not be there were it not for the sudden turbulent rocking of agitated shucks. Then his overalled back appears above the surface of this buff sea, and with arms outstretched he rises, like a tall dark Neptune, gathering within his grasp this sea of shucks. He walks to the darkness of the open doorway of the great barn, carrying securely within his extended hold, for cow bedding, the coverings of hundreds of ears.

But still the tide rises, faster than young Neptune can remove it.

And all this time, while the twenty-five colored people work, the preparing of the feast goes on within the farmhouse. Beef hash, chicken dumplings, potato pudding, potato pies, hot biscuits: food awaits the exhausted bodies, food to be served in relays at white cloth-covered tables decked with pickles and preserves, food to be handed round by women in gay-colored prints and smoothed oiled hair. For the corn shucking is a high point in the year's rituals, and its celebrants shall pay it due honor.

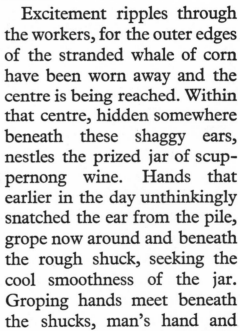

Excitement ripples through the workers, for the outer edges of the stranded whale of corn have been worn away and the centre is being reached. Within that centre, hidden somewhere beneath these shaggy ears, nestles the prized jar of scuppernong wine. Hands that earlier in the day unthinkingly snatched the ear from the pile, grope now around and beneath the rough shuck, seeking the cool smoothness of the jar. Groping hands meet beneath the shucks, man's hand and woman's hand, and pause and feel the warmth of finger and palm, before withdrawing to the business of the day. But still the cold smooth jar eludes them, and the sun crosses the heavens beneath the film of grey cloud.

"If'n Jim Burney's gone and deceived us this time we'll never come and shuck for him again," shouts the young man with the khaki cap turned back to front, as he fumbles beneath the corn for the hand of the girl beside him, the soft warm girl with the tight little plaits of hair over her head and the dress as bright blue in color as a stained-glass window in a church. But he knows the whole time that the little fingers hold more magic for him than any jar of scup wine.

Jim Burney smiles. He could tell exactly where that jar is hidden. His smile strokes all these friends gathered around him, these folks who go from farm to farm to help their neighbors. Yes, he feels good today, Jim Burney does. He feels mighty good, for only yesterday a white man from near by had come and asked him if'n he wouldn't sell his farm, this farm that had been given him by his own pappy. And he'd offered him big money, too, that white man had. Jim's gentle eyes pass over the group of friends around him, to the great cedar tree beyond the rail fence. "Fifteen years ago I could bend it and snap it with a penknife, and I don't mean for it ever to be cut down," he tells himself. And in his mind his great limbs stride his fields and his long arms pick tobacco and cotton. His eyes pass back from the tall cedar tree to his eldest son, the young Neptune rising from the sea of shucks, and he knows that the white man's money means nothing. This is his own earth, and it shall remain so. Nobody can take it from him.

But there is commotion. The jar of scuppernong wine has been found. And now no ringing of the dinner bell can call the shuckers in to eat. The stone jar is passed around, leaving behind it in its course gurgles of dark laughter. It should be corn liquor, I feel. As a form of imitative magic it should be corn liquor that they drink, even as we drank the red wine in Saint-Clair at the treading of the grapes. And when the men take to singing after dinner, singing when they have disappeared from the womenfolk in little clumps behind the big barn, I like to think that they have obeyed this oldest of beliefs and have been true to their heritage.

43

"Lord, remember me," they sing, and their voices rise above the brittle thud of the falling ear, the rustle of the shucks.

And then it is over. The shucking is over for one more year. It seems to happen so suddenly, for a few minutes earlier the mottled corn still stood in a diminished clump. But the last ear has spun through the air and twenty-five Negroes rise from chairs and wooden benches, upturned tin baths and sack-covered baskets, leaving the great stretching pile of pale yellow ears to be cribbed later by the family.

Around the well they gather, quenching their thirst before they leave. As the last words of their song echo still from the cedar grove beyond the farmyard, Uncle Silas mounts his mule, to ride to his home across the pines; and the muddy, rutty lane is filled with snorts and roars of old cars, taking back to their cabins and their farms the dusky helpers.

All that is left of today's shucking is a silent farmyard, piled high with pale ears of corn and upturned kitchen chairs, while greedy hens and turkeys peck among the loosened grains upon the ground. Once again the harvest of the earth is gathered into the shelter of the farmyard, for animal and bird and man.

OLD OLLIE

HAS a mean face, I has. It's this selfish look on my face that follows me ever'where; and I can't never leave it, and it don't signify nothin'."

Old Ollie sat on the steps of her back porch, in the shade of the chinaball tree. It was the time of blossoming, and the tree was sprinkled with clumps of frail flowers, delicate mauve in color, centred with long stamens of dark purple. But Ollie was noticing nothing of the beauty around her. She did not see the fling of pink primroses upon the ground, or the flaming scarlet of the pomegranate in bloom. Beyond her fence a great magnolia opened its flowers. The hedges were sprayed with scented honeysuckle.

Old Ollie was aware of none of this. She sat huddled upon the steps, a basket of hog feed by her side.

"There's a certain the sun seems to draw the miseries out of you," she muttered. "And it do be needed, for I feel all puny-like for some days."

She looked up at me as if searching for pity. But I knew what was coming: today was an anniversary.

"My first husband he gone and died ten years ago this very mornin'; but Lord bless you, honey, he do still come and bear down upon me some days till it's as if my heart would bust in my breast. And Mis' Ellen that I used to work for, she would say, 'What's come over you, Ollie,' and I tells her: 'Mis' Ellen, hit's no good, my husband has dunned me, and I'm so lonely in the world that I'd be happier if I was gone and buried under the earth.' Honey, that husband of mine he did treat me like I was a li'l child—and me as couldn't never carry my babies and they would all drop from me."

45

The sun broke through the heavy leafage of the chinaball tree and shone on the old colored woman's two gold teeth. It blazed upon her solitary gold earring, till a confusion of little suns sparkled against the scraggy neck. She shook her head as she talked, and the little suns shifted and swung.

"In my chillun time I was happy," she went on in her slow drawl, "but bit by bit the Lord has tried me out. I suppose hit's because I lost all my folks and two husbands that anyone not kind to me it sort of puts a grief on me. When my mammy was took they was two years keepin' me alive. And then when my granny was took it was just like the Lord had done me wrong, and I would fling my arms over my head and cry to the Lord."

She rocked from side to side upon the step, throwing her thin arms high in the air above her head.

"I love kindness," she moaned. "I love kindness so mighty much that anybody can kill me with it. When you're kind to me I work myself to death. And it makes me happy when I work like that. My old mammy made me work since I was jest big enough to tote a flour poke full of cotton, and her a whacking woman with that great poke on her back. That sun never rose on my old mammy in bed. Lawsy no, honey, hit never did rise on her in bed."

It seemed to me that Ollie was more upset than usual by her anniversary. I wondered what had happened.

"Shouldn't you be working this morning, Ollie?" I asked her. "Oughtn't you to be way out at Mis' Ellen's?"

She broke down and sobbed.

"Yes, indeedy," she bawled. "Hit be that what have put a grief on me. Mis' Ellen she say to me, Ollie,' she done say, 'Ollie, you's too old now to work. You's to go home and rest.' And me what's worked all my life since my chillun time. So I sets and I sets, and all I can do is to go and collect feed for my hawgs—jest like all the ol' nigger women around. I go along the streets to the garbage cans when the garbage man has done come and put the cans in the front of the yard, befo' they gits them emptied into the trucks, and I picks out the ol' bread and cakes and puts them in my basket for my hawgs. You'd best step up and see my hawg feed."

She dragged me after her into the back kitchen, where the feed stood in baskets and cartons. Three mice scampered away as we came close. A line of torn washing hung across the room; but against the small window rested the sunlit leaves of her little fig tree. She saw me turn towards the fig tree, and the ugly old face smiled.

"That li'l fig tree and my hawgs, they're my only friends now," she drawled. "They and the chinaball tree and the peach out in the yard. For I done lost all my folks and I don't belong nowhere. Now, in the days of my gran'pappy and my granny folks weren't never so lonesome, for folks belonged. Yes, honey, folks belonged."

Suddenly I understood what she meant. I looked at the broken old Negro woman and knew that I talked with the grandchild of a slave, and a grandchild who neither wanted nor understood freedom.

"I suppose if I could read or write I wouldn't be so lonesome," she went on. "For then I could read all what the Lord says in the Good Book. But when I gets specially lonesome for my folks I sometimes has a notion to go up and see where they is; and then it all comes over me that I never knew where my home was or where my folks come from. My gran'pappy in my chillun days told me how when he were a young un way back in slavery, he would creep off to other plantations to see the girls, so when the time come he was freed he couldn't never get to feel safe on the road but would walk through the swamps—yes, even if'n it took him way off his path. Lord, Lord, honey, my gran'pappy he couldn't never get used to bein' freed."

"And your granny?" I asked her. "How did she take it?"

"My granny she'd been sold same as she was cotton or corn. But she were younger when she were freed, and she jest stayed on and nursed them li'l white chillun, so that the white chillun, she tells, they would come and visit her and she knowed she belonged. And

she and Aunt Fanny and Aunt Susie, they was happy, they was."

I looked about me at the grim little back kitchen. Over the mantel stood a shabby frame, and in it was a newspaper photograph of a smart young colored man.

"But who's that?" I wanted to know, for he did not seem to fit into the picture I had formed of Old Ollie's world. He was of a different civilization, and in his face I saw an expression of defiant freedom. Here was young Negro America.

The old woman smiled sadly as she answered me.

"That?" she said. "Why, that's Ebenezer, that is. No, he ain't exactly what you might call one of my folks, though he were brought up by my ol' mammy. When the floods come out in Montgomery and we was in the time of 'struction, my mammy found a baby way high up out of them waters; and, she tuck that boy baby home with her and raised him till he were 'most a grown man. But he had ideas that wasn't like ours, and he weren't never happy with us. And then one day he runned off from my ol' mammy, and we heerd he'd gone to the city and worked his way through school. We never heerd of him again—no, not even when my ol' mammy was buried. But one day when I was at Mis' Ellen's I sees his picture in the paper that was wrapped around some meat for the little dog and I calls Mis' Ellen. 'Mis' Ellen,' I say, 'I cayn't neither read nor write, but if you would tell me what the name is that's written under this picture I'd sho' be mighty glad.' And Mis' Ellen she says, 'Why, Ollie,' she says, 'his name is Ebenezer Jefferson.' 'Ebenezer Jefferson,' I cries, and I comes over all quare and puny-like. And Miss Ellen she says his picture was in the paper because as he was become a big teacher. But he don't belong to me no mo', honey. No, he don't belong to me no mo'."

She had opened the door to the back porch, and we sat side by side on the rickety steps.

Her hand fumbled in a pocket of her apron and brought out a small tin box. She opened it and placed a pinch of snuff in her lower lip.

"Hit's a pacifier, hit is," she said. "Hit's a pacifier so that I can work."

But I felt that even as she said it she knew that the cotton fields would see her no more, and that a spruce young colored girl stood at the sink in Mis' Ellen's kitchen and the little white children of the house were already forgetting her name.

"I 'spects hit's the mean look on my face," she drawled. "Nobody never knows how I loves kindness. Nobody never knows how I'd work myself to death for them—so only I'd have somewhere to belong. For there ain't nothin' so lonesome in the whole world as not to belong."

As I left her I had a vision of three figures. An aged Negro stumbled along the swamps, among the cypress knees, his terrified eyes searching the mist of Spanish moss for spectre slave owners; a young colored teacher stood before his class, and as he talked with the students he saw a procession of the Negroes of the future, lawyers and doctors, steelworkers and scientists. But the third figure was the one that haunted my eyes: it was an old woman with a basket of hog feed. She gazed at the aged Negro as he stumbled among the cypress knees, and turned then to the young colored teacher with the fire of defiance in his face. But loneliness was upon her. She did not belong.

SPRING IN THE CAROLINAS

THE redbirds knew it was coming long before we humans could feel any stirrings in the air. They knew it each day at sunrise, and saluted it with disquieting fervor. Morning after grey morning, while the earth was cold still and hard, the redbirds sang their shamelessly seductive love songs. They sang with ardent certainty, while it needed an act of faith for us to believe that there could ever again be spring.

Then there came the day when the imminence of spring pierced our duller sensibilities. There came the day when suddenly we could understand the hardness of the earth in the woods beneath our feet. Like a woman great with child, this earth we stepped upon would burst at any moment and break into leaf and blade, bud and flower. The skin was stretched tight across its body; this that we trod was a fecund hardness. And in one of those rare moments of insight into reality, we knew that the barriers between man and plant could fade and we waited on the birth of a flower even as we await the birth of a child. In this spirit we watched the surface of this taut skin in the darkness of the woods, searching for the first crack in the earth, the first green blade.

Any day now, we knew, any day now it might come.

And then it happened. It did not happen gently as in England, but with the sudden violence that characterizes the American continent. The stretched skin broke under the urgent strain of the little blossoms, and the world of the Carolinas surrendered to spring.

Scenting the blooms of the bushes of sweet-breath-of-spring, gazing at the quaker-ladies at my feet, I thought of the timidity of the springs I had known, with snowdrops shaking in the cold east winds and pale primroses flowering in the shelter of English lanes.

Here I was to watch something completely new.

Come slowly, I felt like begging of it. Give me time to watch these unfamiliar buds swell and unfold.

But the force of growth is so violent that nothing will wait. The sudden soft warmth of the air lures the bud from the sheath, the leaf from the mold. My stumbling mortalness fails to keep pace with this power surrounding me. While I try still to encompass the foam of the flowering plum I see that the first buds have burst on the peach trees in the garden beneath me, where but a few days back there had been as yet no sign of swelling.

People had told me of spring in the Carolinas. They had tried to describe the voluptuous abandon of it, the wanton beauty that draped the trees and garmented the earth. In my mind I saw pictures of the flowering meads of the Italian Primitives. Primavera scattered blossoms over everything. I gazed again at a pink sea of peach trees against the blue and silver of the Mediterranean and flings of wild freesia upon the mountain sides of Provence. Violets purpled the islands of the Aegean and I trod with care upon the carpet of dwarf crocuses that stretched to the water's edge in Corsica, or lay among the sweet-scented narcissi in the South of France. I walked in English woodlands, sulphur with primroses, smoky with the drifts of bluebells. I filled my mind with the remembrance of all the blossomings that I had ever seen. Chronicled and sung through the centuries, wreathed into chaplets of verse by Greek poets, these hyacinths and narcissi, these violets, crocuses, and primroses had decked the hair of the gods. But always, it seemed to me, when I remembered them, the flowers were enriched by legend or association. Here, now, in this new world, they would be drenched clean for me of emotion. Here I should discover beauty that was as yet unsung and form that could be loved for itself alone.

With excitement I awaited this spring.

But what I wanted to learn was the shapes of the little unknown flowers that grew in the woods and the meadows. Soon, I knew, the gardens of the Deep South would be flung open to the public, and spectacular masses of flaming azaleas would hold the eyes of the world; while all unnoticed, in the woods, in the secret places, small things would be pushing through the earth. These were the flowers I sought.

And these were the flowers that I found. The first knobs of buds on the hepatica plants, the first bloodroot, the first dogtooth violet in the woods by the dam, springing up among the crisp dead leaves that clasped it and enfolded it and seemed as though they would draw it down into the earth with them, to crumble and rot. Looking at this first dogtooth violet, I felt that I watched in microcosm the entire struggle of life.

But soon these small flowers were caught up in the surge of growth, and where one had had to search closely to find them, for else the woods seemed dead and still, and brown and empty, now the ground was bright with stretches of color.

This power of spring is so strong that seeds germinate and sprout within a few days, and trees thicken at their tips before one's eyes. The sense of growth is so insistent that it overpowers the mind and, walking through the woods, one becomes oneself earth and trees, sharing in the season. I look down at my finger tips, amazed that they, too, should not be sprouting into bud and blossom and leaf. For it is as though the whole of life were caught into this delirium of growth. And am I not part of life?

Let me belong to it too, I plead. Let me become a part of this alien spring. But my finger tips do not sprout into bud and blossom and leaf, and a strange waywardness blinds me to this voluptuous flowering and sends my mind shooting back to the memory of some straggling, wind-battered plant that I tended in my days of childhood. The Carolina wren sings, "You pretty you pretty you pretty

53

you," and the cardinal says, "Dear—dear—dear"; but they battle in my ears with the senseless cry of the English cuckoo and the sawing love song of my native blue tit, till I grow angry within me at this foolishness.

It is a strange thing, nostalgia. It is a jealous god, resentful of new

happiness. Just now, at this moment, as I turn a corner of the dirt road by John Mangum's farm, where a yellow-wheeled wagon stands under blossoming peach trees, like a painting by van Gogh, and a great buzzard floats in the sky above me, just now, here, in North Carolina, it seems as though I almost belong. The red earth has a purple bloom from the heavy rains, and the raucous green of rye and winter wheat sprouts in curves of contour plowing that accentuate the form of the land. In front of the small grey cabins of unpainted wood that are dotted over the gentle hills of this piedmont country, daffodils run like little creeks of pale gold. Mules frisk in the soft air, and the clean sun of early spring throws upon the cabins the shadows of tree trunks and bare boughs; and these patternings, running out from the trees, bind the frail houses to the earth and give them weight, so that, like little kittens with their toes tucked under them, they rest secure beneath majestic maples and oaks that would seem else to overpower. Now, at this exact moment, it is as though this were my home, and the clean bright sun of early spring binds me, with my own shadow, to the earth of North Carolina.

But it is only for a fraction of a moment. The jealous god of nostalgia watches my mind. Like a fade-out in a movie, the scene before me blurs and I can see no longer the yellow-wheeled wagon under the pink blossoms. I am a child again, in Aunt Sarah's garden, and the brave buds of our solitary peach tree swell slowly and burst with difficulty against the whips of the cold east wind. We gaze at it, I and the little old woman, and I am filled with awe while she tells me again, as she has done countless times, of the day she pushed a peach stone into the earth. With caress in her voice she describes the shoot that cracked the surface of the earth, the growth of the young tree over the years, the day of the sacramental eating of the first ripe peach. Our eyes stroke the tree before us, and upon the vision of our mind is impressed each bough, each twist and turn of trunk. We see it stark against the winter sunset, budding in spring, its leaves turned red in the fall, and as though it were a sundial so we can tell the hour of the day in high summer by the length and angle of the cast shadow. We are filled with love for our peach tree, and know the sound of it, the scent of it, the feel of it. It is the essence of all peach trees. Years later, as I wakened in the train in Provence, and saw from my window for the first time a stretching sea of peach trees, ghostlike in the light of dawn, as yet unflushed by the sun, I knew for a certainty that each tree had the same twist and turn of trunk, the same shape to its boughs, the same buds and blossoms as my own peach in the garden at Swallowfield. So does childhood stamp upon us the pattern for all our life. And so, it would seem, we need

55

to surround each thing we look upon, that we may truly love it, with an aura of personal magic. Proust with his pink hawthorn, I with my

pink peach tree, each man of us with his special memory, in our human frailty we must carry an illumination from within that we shed upon the world. Perhaps we are not big enough in spirit to comprehend absolute beauty.

Thus as we gaze upon the Grand Canyon we are numbed before the impersonal wonder of it, and delight is denied us, to be given for something smaller, like the spear of the first snowdrop above the hard earth. It is not perfection that brings magic, nor abundance, nor immensity; it is something that comes to us suddenly and un-awares. So, as I lie on the ground in South Carolina and look at my first pitcher plants, I know that I am seeing them with precious clarity. I had sought these strange flowers with great difficulty, over many miles, afraid lest they should disappoint me. Exhausted after the glare of azaleas, scared by the evil of the wisteria that, like a predatory creature, leaps the trees as if to strangle them, coiling and twisting in tortured convolutions, as though it were some great land octopus that would suck the life out of its prey, bewildered by the easy abundance of growth here in this land, I lie with relief upon the ground by this single clump of pitcher plants. But here, I know, I have not escaped from the feeling of evil. The whole plant world seems filled with a queer sense of foreboding, till my northern blood craves a bracing wind to sweep away this lush exuberance. Dripping grey ghosts of Spanish moss above and around me, wooing the young leaves of the live oaks that sprout with such defiance, all seems filled with gloom. Spring here has none of the young joy of the English scene, none of the benign light of the Mediterranean. I turn to the clump of pitcher plants; strong pale green of leaf, gleaming yellow of flower, against the tangle of dead grasses they are like a set of dwarf organ pipes. I wait for sound to come from them, and wonder what music would issue from this weird plant. And as I examine the flowers, the buds, the strange leaves, I am fascinated by their form.

Here at any rate I can be free of all association, and can learn these shapes. I finger them, exploring the carnivorous pitcher-shaped leaves, formed with all the wiles of Nature to inveigle insects into their depth. I stroke the wavy yellow petals that hang down from the inverted dome of the flower like thirsty tongues. I hold within my

57

hand the round hard balls of buds. Thus, close to them, touching them, and following their form with my hands, I can learn them. And, learning them so, I know why I am bewildered and unmoved by the profusion of azaleas. I must be content with the color of them, and I am not able to learn their form. It is through the sense of touch that knowledge comes.

I lift my eyes from the pitcher plants, and they rest upon uncurling cinnamon ferns. Here is something that I know well, but something that has the power each spring to excite me anew, as though I had never seen it before. And once more the old struggle starts, between enjoyment of absolute form and delight in the sense of association, and while part of me fingers the rust-colored fruit that backs the fern and enjoys the woolly curled fronds, another part has travelled far from the scene before me, and I stroke ferns in the Lake District in England, or bend to look at spleenwort at the foot of some grave in a village churchyard in Dorset.

But what is happening over there? I am drawn back to South Carolina. Colored children walk the narrow winding path through these woodlands. They walk in single file, like an orderly procession, and on their heads they balance great bundles of firewood. Each child carries a bunch of pink flowers. I look more closely and see that they bear bouquets of wild azaleas,

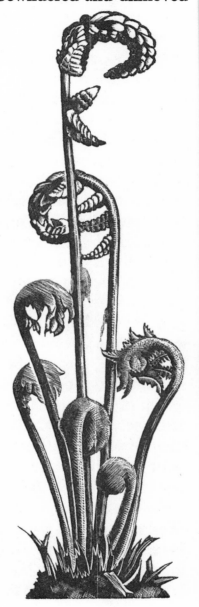

like offerings to some god. As they walk they sing. This, now, is spring, and these children celebrate.

Looking at them as they wind their way among the pitcher plants and cinnamon ferns beneath the festoons of Spanish moss, I see them as the colored brothers and sisters of the children in the England of my childhood, who chose their Queen of the May, decked her with flowers and marched with her through village and town, singing their songs and dancing their dances. I do not know where these colored children are going, but I like to think that something of the magic of this spring morning has entered into them and though they may be homeward bound, to chores and the tending of baby sisters, yet their singing and their bouquets of wild pink azaleas are offerings to the spirit of fertility. And I delight in it, knowing that their joy is a reproach to our deadened senses, and a lesson that we need.

Spring is in the blood of the colored people, and yards are gay with pegged seed packets and the fences and porches of all the Negro cabins are covered with patchwork quilts and clothes that have been hung in the sun to air. As some may sing and dance in celebration of the coming of spring, these colored people have their own ways of giving tribute. Search the countryside on Easter Monday, and it is desolate. But go to any small bridge, any lake, or creek, or running stream, and you will know why the stores are closed and nobody is at work. Leaning over tiny bridges, crouching on the banks of creeks or rivers or running streams, they are there, the colored people, in their scores. They fish, but it is not for what they may catch. "It's not that I wants to catch anythin'," old Jerry Baker tells me. "It's that I likes to feel the fish bite. I likes jest to set on the river bank and feel them bite, all the day long." So, throughout the evenings of spring, till the fish start to "play" and the law forbids anyone to catch them during the breeding season, the colored folk sit and watch the buds swell and the leaves grow upon the trees, while they hold in their hands a fishing rod. But though the hands may hold the rod and would feel the tug of the fish when it bites, yet their eyes learn the coming of spring.

I watch this unfamiliar spring. By the dam I see at my feet a shed snake skin; it is complete and perfect, and the transparent eye coverings gaze at me as I lift it. Little strange lizards dart along the hot rocks, and the bright blue of the tail of one, and the brilliant green on the back of another, and the peacock blue down the chest of yet another look like clumps of precious stones among the grey rocks. I am surrounded by unknown creatures. Orange-splashed turtles sun themselves on the logs of felled trees that lie across the river. Above me on the topmost branch of a tulip poplar tree sings a mockingbird, and so intense is his ecstasy that it is not enough to sit there on the highest bough; he must leap into the air in excess of emotion, carrying his song yet higher with him, two feet, three feet higher than the tip of the tallest tree. Again and again he makes his singing leap, till it is like ecstasy made manifest. Or the quiet of the privet bush is suddenly shaken by a swarm of cedar waxwings, greedily eating the berries. As the sun catches the bands of yellow at the tips of their tails, it is as though they had brushed against the petals of some early jonquils in their dipping flight and had carried them into the air with them.

But most of all I delight in my first sight of white egrets. I cross the South Santee River, and the banks of the muddy water are dotted with these birds, their thin bodies reflected in the river. Here, as I watch them closely, I know that I am seeing absolute beauty. Beneath me, in the shadow of the bridge, an egret stretches himself, and the long neck stands straight above the graceful body. His nuptial feathers hang down around him, for it is spring. And then the neck curves and bends, and the great white wings open and lift the bird into the air. He vanishes down the river, a lope in his flight. This variety of movement has not lacked beauty for one fraction of a moment. As he disappears from sight I find myself wishing that I could live always with such beauty, as a stronghold against the discord of life.

But though my egret may have flown, other beauty surrounds me. The banks of the highway are dotted with tiny wild purple iris. I pick one, and its scent is sweet. Farther down the road I see a blur of blue, and when I come closer it turns into a spreading clump of wild lupine. Looking at them in wonder, I remember the sudden sight of a field blue with grape hyacinths, in North Carolina. In amazement I had told people of my discovery, supposing it to be something of importance, and I was yet more surprised to find that the grape hyacinth, prized with such care in England, was considered here as little more than a weed. "Bluebottles, you mean?" asked some one. "Why, they're nothing but weeds." And I thought then of the crimson and yellow wild columbine in the woods of Maryland, and of the white columbine in the Rocky Mountains; I saw in my mind wild larkspur and a profusion of orange day lilies. And I had again the same feeling of guilty luxury that I always have here in America when I see in abundance, growing wild and untended, these little flowers that grow in England so sparsely and that we cultivate with such care.

But all this time that I look about me at this spring, trying to make it my own, and to be absorbed into it, I know that something is lacking. The fret of nostalgia comes between me and the beauty of the woods as I walk among budding dogwood trees. Desperately I try to wrench myself from this senseless longing for my English earth. I look down at the green stars of young gum tree leaves, at the bright yellow of cinquefoil, at the closed pink fist of wild honeysuckle. A little creek runs through these woods; butterflies hover in the sunlit air. "The whole earth is your garden," I tell myself. "The entire world is your spring." But the deadness and the fret persist, a cataract over the eyes of my spirit.

And it is then that it happens. Like a revelation I know what is wrong. I am an outsider because I am a spectator. I have no under-standing of this spring because I have no share in it. Suddenly I know why my mind swings back from this lush exuberance to the straggling, wind-battered plants of my English garden. I leave the woods and walk down the street to the nearest ten-cent store. There, in a little packet costing one dime, stands my open-sesame. Tenderly I prepare the earth in my window box, and sprinkle upon it the seed from this little packet. I wait over the days in suspense and excite-ment. And then, one morning, I see that the surface of the earth is woven into a pattern of little cracks, and at midday, drawn up by the light of spring, tiny green seedlings pierce these cracks and face the sun of the Carolinas. I look at the seedlings with gratitude, knowing that they have the power to illumine for me each tree and each flower. For by grace of these tiny shoots, I am no longer an outcast. Suddenly I belong.

FLOOD

T WAS early in July, too, that it had happened last year. I shall never forget the look of terror on Sam Barnley's face as he shouted across the meadow. His cry was caught up and flung from man to man, from farm to farm:

"The river's out of the banks!"
"The river's out of the banks!"
"The river's out of the banks!"

The cry leapt across space, and was handed on like a torch in battle.

It started a few Sundays ago, with a thunderstorm. We were swimming in the James River, and the heat was hardly bearable. We ducked our heads beneath the mud-colored water, hoping in vain to store some of its coolness. The water itself seemed sticky and warm; the wet upon our bodies turned to sweat as soon as we were above the surface of the river.

"It's time we went back," Delia kept repeating.

But still we stayed in the water, knowing that between us and the cool of the farmhouse lay the shadeless heat of the low grounds. Up the river bank we should have to drag our weariness, up the river bank and across the strip of corn to the old shed where we kept our boat. We knew how we should linger there in the shade of that broken-down shed, seeking excuses to look at the harrow or the plow or the rotting boat that we used to have before we saved up and bought this new one. And Delia would draw little Tommy to her, and lift him on the harrow, for a ride, while she wiped the sweat from her forehead, where it was dripping into her eyes and making them smart. But we liked to pretend that we were hardened farmers, and not just newcomers here, and we never confessed to each other how we feared that long stretch of low ground before us, that stretch of blazing earth that turned and reeled beneath our feet, that earth that seemed at times as if it would rise up and hit us.

This particular Sunday was worse even than usual for July. There was a strange heaviness in the air that pulled us down to the ground. The atmosphere had the sullen uneasiness of the tropics, and one expected to see alligators raising their heads above the muddy waters of old James.

We managed at last to pull ourselves together enough to swim to our boat, and when I had got Delia and the two children inside it I hauled them down the river myself, wading through the channels that were shallow. The sun beat down upon me, but my legs and thighs were cool beneath the water. It seemed as though the sky had turned a muddy yellow, till you could scarcely tell sky from river. The river was low, I remember thinking; there was no risk of flood this year. I had a terror of flood all through me, for I had lost most of my corn last summer, and a whole field of soya beans had been destroyed. That flood had nearly ruined me, coming as it did the year I had bought this farm, when I had had to put out so much money on a new tractor. Yes, I remember thinking with relief that the river was low.

"Not much fear of a flood this year, Delia," I had called to my wife. "The river isn't more than two or three feet deep just here. Tommy might almost come in and haul with me, if he has a mind to."

We weren't far from our mooring place when it happened. It happened with all the force of a tempest in the Scriptures. And it seemed to come from nowhere, for there wasn't as yet a cloud in the sky. It was a great wind that bent the trees and whipped the James River into slashing sheets of water. It drove me before it, till I almost fell. It dashed our boat upon me, and the prow banged my thighs till they bled. We couldn't have been more than a dozen yards by now from the mooring place, but that stretch of leaping water filled me with terror. If only the branches of the willow trees don't snap before we get past them, I remember thinking. If only no tree trunk falls across our boat, we shall be all right.

I did not dare to pause and look up at the sky behind me, but Delia tells me that suddenly, with the wind, a great black mass of cloud had risen in the west and was racing across the heavens. She shouted to me, she says, to hurry; but the wind must have caught her words and carried them above and beyond me, for they never reached my ears.

I staggered through the swirling waters, and at last reached the mooring place. I made Delia and the children lie flat on the ground while I dragged the boat into the shelter of the overhanging bank. But even here, I saw, it would not be safe, for the waters whirled and lapped and sucked and splashed till very soon the boat would have been battered to bits.

I don't know how I managed to haul that boat up the bank and across by the strip of corn to the shelter of the old shed. I believe that one is capable of some strange strength in moments like this. The long loose leaves of corn cracked like sharp whips. The blown earth stung my face and beat into my eyes till I was almost blinded. I can remember running back to fetch Delia and the children, and dragging Tommy beside me in the lee of my body, while Delia took care of Emmie. I can remember falling with Tommy under me, and swearing at him when he started yelling. At times it was all so hard that I wondered if it would be wiser just to lie down there in the corn, even if it meant being whipped and slashed by the corn leaves. But the great black mass of clouds was covering the sky and rumbles of distant thunder could be heard, even above the roar of the hurricane. And I knew that we had to get home to the cellar.

We did it. We made our way across the low grounds, past the persimmon sprouts that I'd never yet had time to grub off, across the railroad track as far as the sheep barn. I had never before realized how many gates we had to latch and unlatch, to keep the cattle in—

though, when I come to think of it, I never for one moment then remembered the cattle. I suppose they were somewhere around there in the pasture, but I was so concerned with Delia and the children

that I didn't look about me. We reached the farmhouse just as the first drops of rain were starting to fall, and the lightning was beginning to blind us and illumine the dark countryside.

All that evening the rain fell, from midday until we were in bed. It fell with a savagery that was evil. It slashed at the window of our bedroom, and poured in torrents from the leaves of the oaks in the grove before the house. The wind had died down. There was now neither thunder nor lightning. Only the rain fell.

Next morning there were gleams of sun; but by midday exactly the same thing happened again. A crazy wind rose with unbelievable suddenness, and the sound of that wind in the trees was just as if a great rainstorm were beating down upon them. The wind kicked the leaves from the trees, and tossed them against the windows of the house, or whirled them in little eddies in the air.

It wasn't long before the rain started again—just as it had started the day before. But this time it fell with even greater force. It was as if the skies had opened and emptied themselves upon the earth. You could see nothing beyond the nearest oak trees in the grove, and the wooded hills were hidden in a steely sheet of falling water. The rain fell all that day, and ironically we were out of drinking water. "We'll have to do without any if it goes on like this," I had said to Delia. "Nobody could ever reach the spring in this blinding storm." But little Emmie was thirsty with the heat, and started crying: and so what could I do? I tore down the lane, and if I hadn't known the way so well that I could have found the slope that leads to the spring even if I'd been blindfolded, I'd never have seen it, for the rain was like a tent of wet steel around me. I could hear the waters of the creek tumbling over the rocks—the little creek that crawls along so lazily during the summer months, the little creek where we go down and bathe ourselves and it isn't too deep for Emmie to stand in. It must have been rushing, for it was roaring like a great waterfall, so that I could hear it even above the downpour of the rain.

We had these thunderstorms, with ceaseless rain, every day for nearly a week—that strange wind rising suddenly at midday out of an ink-colored sky with thunder and lightning. Delia began to get afraid of flood, but I reminded her that the river had been lower than usual when the rains began.

"Sam Barnley says it isn't up more than a few feet," I told her. "It could rise quite a bit more and there'd be no danger."

But all this time countless tiny streams far away were swelling as they rushed down the mountain sides. Little sluggish trickles were being fed by the dripping leaves upon the trees and by the soaked earth among the rocks, till they became fast-running and angry. Drops of water that usually fell indolently from barely dampened ledges became turbulent waterfalls. Dry rocks were hidden beneath foaming, gurgling eddies. And lower down the mountain sides, where the feeding streams were wider and deeper, little wooden footbridges were being submerged and swept away by the force of the hurrying waters.

Cowpasture River; Bullpasture River; Calfpasture River; each gathered into itself the turbulent offerings of the upland streams, ochre with the muddy earth of the Blue Ridge Mountains; and upon the surface of the waters floated twigs and branches and small tree trunks that had been wrenched from their growing places in the high lands. Pedlar River, Buffalo River, Rockfish River—they hurtled their swollen waters into the James.

And the rains fell. With grey persistence they fell, long after the thunderstorms had ceased. Relentlessly they fell, day after day after day, till the house grew sodden with damp and clothes and books were limp. We dreaded the journey to the well at the back of the house and drew lots as to which should go down the lane to the spring for drinking water.

But still I felt I could truthfully state that there was no risk of flood.

I know it was my fault that it happened as it did; there was no one else to blame for all the trouble I had. I thought at the time that Sam Barnley might have reminded me of the cattle; but I believe that he had a contempt for me as a newcomer, and I have to admit that I had declared all along that there would be no flood, the river being so low to start with. Anyhow, the day came when the rain actually stopped and we saw the sun again. It was in the middle of the afternoon that it started to clear and there was a sky full of stars when we went to bed.

But what I had forgotten was that it took quite a while for all those countless mountain streams, all those tributaries—Cowpasture, Bullpasture, Calfpasture and Buffalo—to flow into old James.

It was greying to dawn when I was wakened suddenly by the sound of gravel being thrown against our window; and then I heard Sam Barnley's voice calling me:

"Mr. Wilbur, the river's out of the banks. You'd best come down to the low grounds, or the water mought get the cattle."

It didn't take me long to dress. We ran down the lane and across the road to the sheep barn, and I took time to snatch up the wooden handle of a grubbing hoe, thinking I might be needing it with the animals. It was just as we crossed the railroad tracks that I saw what had happened. You may remember that there's a dip in the land there, so that it is a much lower level all the way over to the river itself. The whole stretch of low ground was transformed into a great lake.

"The cattle," I gasped. "Where's the cattle?"

In the half-light of pre-dawn we could hardly see. Hopefully I searched the water before me for the great black shapes.

"They're over there, by the far fence," called Sam. "Yonder where the land's a slight bit higher. I can't count them from here, but it would seem to me from the size of the mass that they're about all of them together."

We stared at this lake below us, and then at each other.

"I'll do it," I said. And I plunged into the dark water, the wooden hoe handle in my left hand. The flood must have come above my armpits, for none of the persimmon sprouts showed on the surface of the water.

69

Suddenly I remembered the calves and I knew there would be little hope of saving them.

I struck out. There was no time to waste, for the waters were still rising and soon the island of high land would be submerged. I struck out towards them, and as I swam my feet caught in the branches of the persimmon sprouts.

"The fence," I warned myself. "Keep well away from the barbed-wire fence."

Then—I must have been about halfway across these flooded low grounds—there came to me a frightening sound. Louder than the flood waters was the bawling and bellowing of the cattle. Hearing this, in a flash I remembered being told by a cow hand out West that there was nothing on earth so awful as the terror of cattle in fire or blizzard or flood. Fire or blizzard or flood. Fire or blizzard or flood. Flood. Flood. Flood. Like a person going off under an anaesthetic, I heard this word repeated, over and over till it became the sound of the waters gurgling against me as I swam. Louder and louder in my ears was this bellowing of the cattle, so completely different from the mooing of hunger or thirst. It was a sound I had never heard in my life before, and my own terror began to equal that of the beasts I was to save.

If only the sun would rise, I felt; if only I could see what was happening, it wouldn't be so terrifying. But I could not wait for dawn; the waters were still rising.

At last I reached the island of high land and clambered up the sopping earth, slipping with each step I took. And then, as I saw this nightmare of a madman before me, my fear took definite form. I knew now what my terror had been. In the dim light of pre-dawn, on the small space of this little island of high land, the great black forms of my cattle milled around, weaving in and out in a panic, bellowing as they trampled upon anything that came their way. I could feel this sense of panic even as I could hear it. And I knew, too, that at any moment I might be the one to be trampled to death. I stumbled over the small body of a calf as I clambered up the bank, and the silence of this little lump told me that it no longer breathed.

The waters were still rising. Something must be done. Then I remembered the cow hand and his tales of flood, and I knew why, without conscious knowledge, I had paused to bring with me the wooden hoe handle. It was no earthly use trying to get behind the cattle and scare them into the flood waters. One small human creature was of little strength against the mass terror of these great unreasoning bodies. I knew that I must get to the front of the milling animals nearest to the water's edge and seize upon one of the cows. I must seize upon her as she passed me in her stampede and grasp her by the tail. I must create a terror in the beast even greater than the terror of this flood. So I seized upon one of the animals, and knowing that the tail was a rudder, twisting this tail I forced her to turn her head towards me. With all the strength that remained in me I cracked her over the nose with the wooden stick I carried. Again and again I beat at her, with such violence that, to the wretched beast, the dark waters of the flood were less frightening than these cracks upon her sensitive nose. She plunged into the blackness before her, and seemed completely to sink beneath the waters. The great body rose in terror and struggled back to land, but I cracked her again on the nose as she began to make for the high ground and once more she sank into the surging flood waters. If I could only keep her in the water I knew she would be all right, for instinct would guide her home, across that dark stretch to where Sam Barnley waited. . . . She had started swimming, and, listening, I could hear her above the sucking sound of the milling cattle as they drew their feet up from the deep mud, this sound that was like pistons on a starting locomotive; above this sound I could hear the puffs and blows of the poor cow as she started on her epic journey to safety.

For one moment of extra terror I thought of the bull. But in this grudging dim light I could not see which was bull and which was cow. All were merged into one great mass of panic, and I also knew that this same panic had robbed the bull of his pride of sex, and that he would be as harmless as a six-weeks calf and as frightened as the rest.

Again and again I seized upon the tail of one of the beasts, beating at it across the nose, till in desperation it took to the waters. The stick broke and was worn down to a nubbin, while yet there were many cattle milling around on this tiny island of safety. In the widening spaces I stumbled upon the bodies of several trampled calves, and wondered, in the few lucid moments out of my desperation, if any had been saved to me. At that moment I heard woven into the sucking sound of the cattle as they drew their feet up from the deep mud, and into the lessening bellow of the frightened beasts, as more and more of them followed their comrades into the dark waters, the bawl of a calf.

All my instincts were roused, to preserve this one calf. I wound my way among the few remaining animals, to where this bawl came from. It was not hard, for by now the great mass of the cattle had taken to the water and those that remained had heard the bellows of their companions far out in the water and were fast following them, plunging blindly, trustingly, into the black flood. In the dim light I felt for the little creature and found it, half smothered beneath the body of its mother. Conflict controlled the cow; between self-preservation and mother love she remained inactive. I seized her calf and drew it after me to the water's edge, just as the last of the animals was taking to the flood.

But how was I to swim in this heaving sea of bodies, a struggling calf in my arms, a frightened mother cow on my heels? As I reached the water's edge and saw the last cow sinking into the flood I knew suddenly what to do. Desperately I grabbed hold of her tail, that I might be carried along in the stream by the beast. Somehow or other I managed to lodge the calf into the hollow of my left armpit, while

I held for dear life to the tail of the swimming cow. I could feel that I was terrifying the animal, as she began to bellow like a bull; but the instinct for self-preservation was strong within her, and she swam hard. The force of the water in flood pulled me downstream, faster than the cow could swim, and pulling me so it almost had the power to turn her upstream, out of her course. The little calf struggled under my left arm. Behind me I could hear the loud puffs of the mother cow, as she swam almost upon me. Time now seemed endless, stretching into eternity. I was so utterly tired that at moments I think I must have lost consciousness. All I remember is the sudden sound of Sam Barnley's voice, above the roar of flood waters and the bellowing of the cattle. Never has human voice sounded more wonderful, or more sweet.

The sky was greening to sunrise as my feet touched ground. Sam Barnley had fetched a rope and was dragging the bogged-down cattle up the muddy bank, the rope around their horns. They plunged and reared up the bank, pitching and digging their hind legs into the

deep mud. But they seemed to understand, the poor wretches, that they were being helped, and they did all in their power to get above the mud and upon the security of dry ground. Exhausted as my own cattle, I lay on the high land and watched the beasts, their breath coming and going like great bellows, their eyes wide with terror.

I do not know how long it was that I lay there, tired beyond all imagination. I wanted to sleep and to go on sleeping. But suddenly, above the puffing and blowing around me, I was aware of a solitary distant mooing. I looked about at the cattle. I counted

"Twenty—twenty-two—twenty-seven—twenty—no, there's only twenty-seven. It's Midnight that's missing," I called to Sam. "She that's due to calve any day now."

I turned toward the flooded pastures. The waters were pale in the light of the rising sun. I could see nothing. But again I heard the low moo of the cow. My eyes followed the sound.

"She's over there, to the left, at the fur end of the pasture," called Sam. "And it do seem to me there's a little black mass by her side, as though she mought have calved this very night."

I was so utterly tired that I could almost have left Midnight and her calf to their fate; but something within me stirred, and I plunged once more into the swirling waters. It would be nothing near so hard this time, with the light of day breaking, and all the cattle safe now on this side. But I was so utterly, completely tired that I will never know how I managed to reach the tiny patch of unsubmerged land.

Even now the water was lapping at the feet of the cow. Digging my hands deep into the soaked turf, I dragged myself to ground. I spoke to the cow, but she would not move. Instead, she turned her head towards the black mass at her side, and licked the little body. But the calf did not stir.

It was then I understood what had happened, and at that moment of understanding Midnight raised her head and bellowed. It was a yearning, forlorn bellow. It was the loneliest sound I have ever heard.

74

But this was no moment for compassion. I must get the animal back to the high ground as quickly as I could, for the water was still rising. I called her. I tried to drag her away from the dead calf by her side. But it was no good. She would not move. There was only one thing to do. I must bring the dead calf with me. I lifted the limp body and hung it over my shoulders. I plaited the long legs across my chest. The head hung heavy over my left arm. The cord dangled wet and messy against my neck.

It was an odd bellow that the cow gave as she followed me into the whirling flood, fearful lest I should be taking her dead calf from her. Her nose was not more than six inches from the calf. Above the rush of the water I could hear her close behind me always, as I swam, and upon the back of my neck her breath blew hot. From time to time the long legs of the calf caught in submerged foliage, and I had to swim around and back to disentangle myself. But always I was followed by this forlorn bellow and the feel of this hot breath, and all the way to the high ground the water was churned up by the great black body of the cow.

And then, of course, next day the waters fell. Looking at the river now, flowing sluggishly within its banks, you'd never think that anything like this could have happened. It's a deceitful old thing, that James is: yes, a deceitful old thing.

HOG KILLING

THEY stand there, crouched and waiting—waiting until the great black hog shall turn her head towards them. They stand there by the side of the pen, and the autumn air is scented with wood smoke and trees stand bare against a clean blue sky.

I wait with these men. I wait here in Maryland for the abrupt sound of a shot from a rifle. Something within me shrinks from what I shall hear and see. Terror begs me to run from the shot and the blood.

The great black hog must feel her fate, for she crouches at the far end of the pen, her head hidden among the stripped corncobs. It is all so calm, so quiet. Gravely the four Negroes stand against the wooden fence, awaiting the moment to kill.

The air is ripped by the shot from the rifle. With a fury of rush the Negroes leap the low sides of the pen and the knife sticks the hog's throat. Stab, stab, stab. From where I stand I can see the colored man's arm plunge and lift and plunge and plunge again. They are killing the hog. Slower and slower heaves the huge body before me, till death wins and the hog lies still. She will never again wander over the curves of this Maryland earth, or shoulder her young ones from the trough at feeding time. I have a sick feeling in my stomach. How easy it is, this killing, whether it be done sharply with a crimsoned knife, or slowly by the fragment of a bomb! . . . This is what happens when life is torn from the body. This is what lies behind short dull words like "blood" and "death." I try to keep my eyes upon the autumn beauty of this countryside, but the bare trees and the blue of the sky are obscured by a pageant of slaughter.

What is it they are saying? Soft dark words come to me through this vision of war, gentle words that seem to reach me across many seas.

"Hawg ain't dead yet," murmurs a voice near me.

"She's gone now," says another voice. "Yes, she's gone now."

Crimson hands drag the great black body from the pen, blood-stained Negro hands that turn iridescent like polished bronze in the light of the sun. Something nestles close against me. I look down. Gertie, the small colored child, stands beside me. She seeks my arm and hides her head, for comfort, in the folds of my coat. I would protect her if I could from this sight of slaughter. Her hand is cold. "When I sees blood," she whimpers, "when I sees blood and they done kill old Betty, my hands go cold." Her dog leaves her side, drawn to the pen by the scent of blood.

The sacrificial rite has started. Fire, water, blood: from time before recorded history, so has it been. Four ragged Negroes have rolled back the centuries, and primeval man serves his gods. Maryland, the Congo, the creeks of the Arunta, it matters not where; the elements are the same, ageless and unchanging.

They are dragging the body of the great black hog from the pen. Her blood stains the thin snow crimson as it drips from the stuck throat. . . . Blood soaked into the earth of Europe: blood tinting the grey seas of the world where the waters close over torpedoed hulks of ships. It should distress me, the sight of blood, and yet strangely I see beauty in this ceremony.

There is here no hate, I tell myself. This scene before my eyes holds nothing ugly or frightening. Look at the gentle way those Negroes haul the body towards the scalding barrel, where the smoke and steam rise into the still blue air, dimming the forms of the burning logs that heat the water. There is tenderness in their movements, and a deep sense of ritual.

Now the hog is immersed in the barrel of hot water, and the murmur of kind dark voices reaches me above the crackle of the logs.

77

"She's goin' all right. Look at her feet peelin' off. You mustn't let the water get too hot or it'll set the hair."

But what is that fifth figure that comes down the slope from the broken-down barn where the mules are stabled? Surely I have seen her before. She walks with the concern of a handmaiden, slowly and with rhythm, as she balances two kettles of boiling water. Her woollen sweater is ripped at the elbows, her skirt mud-stained and torn; but by reason alone of the grace of her walk she should be among the immortals. This is no earthly woman. This figure serves the gods. And now I know where I have seen her: she has walked in a frieze upon a Grecian temple; she has carried water through the ages, as a white woman in the Mediterranean, as a black woman in an African cave painting, as a handmaiden in the Indus Valley. She is the server for all time.

"Ma," shouts the little Negro child by my side. "They've done killed old Betty. They've throwed her into the barrel and she's coming out all steaming and wet."

The colored woman places the two kettles against the burning logs. She turns to the men as they lift the dripping body to its sacrificial altar. The boards of old wood bend under the weight of the men and their burden. She looks appraisingly at the wet carcass.

"You sho' must get that liver ready for dinner, Zeke," she commands. "There hain't nothing to touch real fresh hawg's liver, and you know that all right."

It's their tenderness, I find myself thinking; it's their tenderness that sanctifies this ceremony and robs it of ugliness and terror. There as that tall Negro leans over—he with the tarpaulin hat that surely saw life once upon a water front—there as he lifts the hog farther across the platform, it is with the gesture of a woman moving her sleeping lover.

Scrape, scrape, scrape; old Betty's coarse hair comes off against the knives, leaving her more and more naked, pinker of color, smoother of skin. Round these teats move the huge rough hands, softly, caressingly, as an act of homage. And a murmur of low voices weaves its sound into the crackle of the logs, into the hiss of the hot water poured upon stubborn ears and feet by the Negro woman, into the satisfied clucking of straying hens as they peck at the blood-stained corncobs upon the ground.

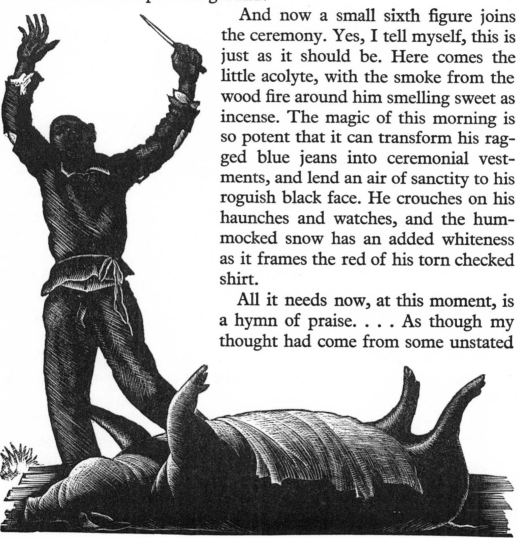

And now a small sixth figure joins the ceremony. Yes, I tell myself, this is just as it should be. Here comes the little acolyte, with the smoke from the wood fire around him smelling sweet as incense. The magic of this morning is so potent that it can transform his ragged blue jeans into ceremonial vestments, and lend an air of sanctity to his roguish black face. He crouches on his haunches and watches, and the hummocked snow has an added whiteness as it frames the red of his torn checked shirt.

All it needs now, at this moment, is a hymn of praise. . . . As though my thought had come from some unstated desire in his breast, the mighty Negro before me straightens himself from the scraping of the hog and stretching his arms with the blood-stained knife above him, lets out a wild dark cry of song. The primitive sounds are caught up by the colored woman, by the three other men, by the small acolyte, by the little child at my side, till the air is filled with an outburst of salutation.

Praise God for the hog, for her liver, for her hams. Praise Him for the rendered lard, for the chitt'lin's and the spareribs. Glory be to God on high for golden corn that she ate, that gave her strength and bulk and meat. Thanks be to Him for the sun and the rain that swelled the corn.

Within me I join in this hymn of praise; but even as I do so I think of the harvest-robbed peasants of the world. It is all wrong, I cry. This is the birthright of each one of us. This culmination of the year's harvests is our due. In this scene of ordered obedience to the seasons lies human sanity. And I see landless peasants the earth over, harvestless and ritual-starved. Between myself and the curling smoke from the wood fire I see Frenchmen torn from their vines, Italians from their farm lands, shepherds from their flocks. I see untended animals whose masters have betrayed them for the care of machine guns. And when the wood smoke thins before me I look upon this human scene with great tenderness, cherishing it as an oasis of content.

"She's sho' ready now for hangin' up," murmurs Zeke. And the waxy body of the scraped hog is trussed and lifted and carried to the foot of the hickory tree.

The sun shines on the opalescent form, and as the men lift it their clear-cut shadows spread across the carcass, accentuating curves that would not else be seen. . . . But what is the little acolyte doing? He has sprung up the tree, and leaps now from branch to branch, coiling into the confusion of the trunks a length of rope. He slings the rope over branches, between trunks, and makes a pulley of the hickory.

They lift and sling the great hog, these four men, moving and hauling and pulling as though they were figures in an ageless dance. It is like a ceremonial measure, where each knows his exact moment, his precise step, his patterned purpose: the men to lift and haul and tug, the woman to wait with the water bucket, the boy to climb and sling and secure the rope. There is not one useless movement, not one unneeded word; the ceremony is as though rehearsed down the years, swinging its way across centuries and cultures. And always, as attendants, stand the unchanging elements of fire and smoke, blood and water.

The hog hangs downward now, from the tree, a swelling pool of crimson beneath her jowl and snout as the blood drains through the corncob plug in her mouth.

"Old Betty, she sho' weighs a mighty deal," says the colored woman as she waits by the trunk of the hickory tree, the bucket of water ready for the ablutions. "Yes, she sho' weighs a lot. I figure the liver will be grand. Yes, I figure it will be grand."

And then, as the next act in this preordained festival, the woman flings the pail of water upon the suspended carcass. It is a sacrificial gesture, a priestly gesture. All conceivable reverence is in that fling of water from an old tin bucket; and the water caresses the form of the hog, glistening in the autumn sun as it drips down to swell the pool of blood at the foot of the tree. Shine of sun upon the wet hog, shine upon the beaded faces of her priests, glitter upon the thin coating of snow that covers the yard; it is a sparkling morning, a fitting day for such blood sacrifice. So lovely is the gleam of water upon that waxy body that I am loath to see the Negro bring forth a cloth and start to wipe the moisture from the hog. Tenderly does he wipe it, though, so that as I watch him I am reconciled to the destruction of those rainbows of light in the water drops. No mother has wiped away her children's tears with greater love, more gracious solicitude. I listen for a lullaby, there is such gentleness in this act.

And the act must have brought some similar thought to his mind, for he straightens himself once again, and this time there is a soft look in his eyes as he talks.

"Do you remember that year, Sarah, when we had to butcher the eight young hawgs? And do you remember how we loved them and the way that they followed us around all over the yard, so that the day of butcherin' I had to go from home, for I couldn't stand it, and we got old Uncle Jeremiah over from the Eastern Shore to kill for us? Now old Betty, I never loved her so much, and yet, as I see her hangin' here, growin' stiff and cold, it seems to me that she had lovely ways with her."

The Negro woman nods her head and murmurs something so low that I fail to hear it. But surely it should have been the word "Amen."

Now, into this gentle praise for the dead, there comes a new sound. It is a rasping sound, piercing the quiet beauty of the eulogy of the hog. The man with the tarpaulin hat and the green trousers sharpens his knives. I look at the scraped, cleaned, wiped carcass and I know what will happen now. There, as I thought; with the artistry of forty butcherings the tall Negro opens up his hog, opens up the drained flesh, discloses the mysteries of life within, coil upon coil, organ among organ, deep red heart, rich bronze liver, each and all of them still, useless, unfunctioning.

By all accounts it should be ugly, this carving of the hog. It should be distressing and ugly. But I watch the Negro woman as she gathers her harvest into the wide tin bath, and I know why I am not disgusted. I watch her as she carries off the treasure to her kitchen, watch her as she balances the tin bath upon her head and, swaying with that walk of the serving-maid of the gods, bears in one hand the longed-for liver.

Today I have seen blood and death, knives and entrails, a rifle and a bullet hole. And yet as I come away, thinking of this blood sacrifice as I look at the bare trees against the clean blue sky, it does not seem to me that beauty has gone from life. I know I have been present at a ritual that was gentle and right, a ritual as old as man, carrying memories of the day when the Primitive Egyptian drew his stone knife across the throat of that animal which was to be at once sacrificed to the gods and fed to the people of the village.

SORGHUM

HE first time I came unexpectedly upon a sorghum mill, in Tennessee, I found myself remembering the day I discovered chair bodgers in an English beechwood. There was the same sense of the unsought, the unexpected. The English beechwood with the thatched workshop hidden among the trees, and the mumble of the two old men as they turned the chair legs on the crudest of lathes, seemed strangely kin to this sudden scene before me. Here in Tennessee I heard a creaking sound, and in a flash of time I was transported to the Chiltern Hills, listening to the primitive lathe worked by the foot treadle that turned the chair legs with such skill that it could compete with the furniture factories. I listened more carefully: nothing, I felt sure, could make such a sound but wood. And it was then that I saw it, in a clearing within the heart of a great clump of trees. And as I saw it, it seemed to me that here was the answer to the idea that all outsiders, all foreigners, have about this American continent. To their way of thinking this is a vast stretch of land so developed that it is given over entirely to mass production, and mass production based to such an extent upon machinery that the hands of man no longer find work to do and the sense of craftsmanship is starved.

I looked at the scene before me, of a sorghum mill as primitive as anything I had ever seen in the most backward regions of Europe, whether it were a well in the Mediterranean island of Majorca, where the blindfolded mules tread the path round the old stone noria that irrigates the countryside, or a cider press in the heart of Devonshire where two old men, endlessly through the days of October, turn the crank that squeezes the juice from the apples of their own orchard.

For this sorghum mill was constructed on the same pattern as one of the primitive wells in Majorca. The similarity extended even to the detail of its being turned by a team of mules. I rubbed my eyes. Was I truly in this new continent of America? I listened, expecting to hear the chant, in the Lydian mode, of one of the ageless work songs of the peasants in the Mediterranean. But here the similarity ended, for there was no song. Instead, a group of colored people shouted and argued, their voices loud above the creak of the long tree trunk that acted as the sweep for the mill.

This, then, was a sorghum mill; this was how the country people made "long sweetenin' or 'lasses," as the mountain folk called it.

Excitement filled me as I watched for the first time an entirely strange craft; it was the same kind of excitement that I had felt when I first saw an Indian woman weaving, or an auctioneer selling tobacco, or an Italian peasant treading grapes. It was the sense of delight in seeing something completely indigenous, about which one as yet knows nothing. And before I knew exactly what I was feeling, I found myself wanting to investigate the mill, to learn precisely why this man sat here, or that cog was fixed there, or what happened when the crushed sorghum juice overflowed the wooden barrel at the other side of the mill, where it stood covered with a tow sack for a strainer, to catch the sticky juice that emerged from the rollers.

The air was sickly sweet with the smell of the crushed cane, and all the flies and wasps and bees of the state of Tennessee seemed to have gravitated to this clearing in the wood, attracted by the scent of sorghum. Behind the mill, beyond the clear circle trodden by the mules, stood a curved, heaped bank. Looking at it from afar, before my eyes had grown accustomed to the strangeness of this scene, I had wondered exactly what vegetation formed this bank; I saw now that it was the accumulated heap of crushed sorghum cane. Sheep strayed over this bank, pausing to lick the sweetness from the cane, and odd followers of this vast army of winged creatures that hovered around the mill alighted upon the nauseating sweetness of the "chews."

But things must now be working more smoothly, for the loud shouting has ceased, and a sweet low song comes from the colored man over towards me, as he gathers together a bundle of sorghum cane and carries it to the mill. He inserts it into the waiting maw as though it were fuel for a furnace, but the alchemy of the mill turns it not into flame but into sweetness, and if I listen carefully I can hear, above the soft, regular tread of the mules that pull the sweep around, and above the rasping sound of metal against metal, the trickle of the syrupy sweetness as it drips out from the mill upon the tow sack, and through the open mesh of the sack into the half-filled wooden barrel beneath.

I begin to understand this primitive craft. It is the same principle as treading, pressing, crushing, sorting, or winnowing, on which all harvests are based. Winnowing beans in Majorca, threshing grain on a mountain side in the French Alps, grinding wheat in an English mill, treading grapes for wine in a Pyrenean village, crushing sorghum cane for long sweetenin' in Tennessee: harvesting is the most completely universal thing in existence. I look with respect at this primitive mill, and suddenly the words of the book of Deuteronomy come into my mind: "No man shall take the nether or the upper millstone to pledge: for he taketh a man's life to pledge." And thinking of this wise verse in the Bible, I feel that the most awe-inspiring things in this world are the tools for man's labor. No matter how primitive they may be, stone upon stone for grinding, curved wood of flail for threshing and winnowing, Indian scraper for skinning pelts, these are the things of beauty that truly matter, above precious stones or empires, and these are the things to be handled with reverence. For they determine the sanity of man's life upon this earth, and he denies them at his own risk.

88

And so as I look at this ramshackle sorghum mill before me, creaking and jamming as it turns, I feel that I look at one of the enduring things of life, and like the Ancient Mariner with the water snakes, I bless it unaware. For here is sanity and here is pride in craftsmanship, without which man cannot healthily live.

But the onlooker might question the pride in craftsmanship as he watches the rough and ready manner in which the cane is shoved into the mill and the crude way it is strained through the tow sack. Let him talk, though, to these men who feed the cane into the mill rolls, and it will not be long before he learns, as we humans always will learn, that behind the simplest procedure lies true knowledge and subtle artistry. Let him talk to that tall colored man over in the far corner of the clearing, as he selects the canes for his bundles. He will tell you that the proper making of sorghum, or molasses, or long sweetening, whichever you choose to call it, depends greatly upon the exact moment of the harvesting of the cane. It should be cut when the seed of the stalk is in the late milk stage. Should you cut it too soon, the syrup will taste uncured and green: should you be delayed and cut it late, when the seeds have gone hard, there will be too much starch in the cane and the syrup will be more difficult to clarify and will probably scorch. If you appear interested he will continue to talk and will tell you that the wise man watches the weather, for should it be too hot and dry the moisture content of the cane is low and the syrup is thick and unyielding. And, in his drawling voice, he will explain that you must surely cut your cane before there is danger of frost, else strange things happen to it and it goes all bad. He doesn't know exactly why, but there it is. All he knows is that you get to feel the day when you've got to cut it, and that he prefers to do his harvesting by hand and has no use for those who won't trouble to remove the side leaves before cutting, but wait to strip them later. And the seed heads? Why, you leave them in the field, of course, to be gathered for feed for the animals. And, so, listening to him, one understands the strange-looking cane stalks, denuded of leaf and seed head, that stand stark in the fields like an impoverished army.

But this that I watch, the cane being fed into the mill rolls, this is not all. Into the sticky sweet scent of the crushed juice is merged the smell of wood smoke. By the rail fence at the far end of the bank of "chews," the highest point of artistry is centered. For there, over the wood fire, in a series of shallow wide tin pans, or evaporators, the juice is boiled. No French cook has developed the master touch more subtly than have these rough colored men as they bring the sticky liquid to the boil, and skim it, and again skim it, tossing to the ground the ladled impurities that rise to the surface in the boiling. The air is a hum of insects, the ground where the scum lies tossed is dim with winged creatures, and the dirty frothy scum itself is speckled with the black bodies of overeager flies and bees and wasps that have drowned themselves in the boiling liquid or passed to death in the crushing maw of the mill. Like the purification of a spirit, getting nearer and nearer to perfection, the boiled juice passes from evaporator to evaporator, and with each advance toward completion the syrup grows deeper in color and thicker in substance, till, in the end pan, near the chimney, it lies thick and clear, a deep warm greenish brownish yellow syrup, ready for storing.

But this, I feel as I watch the lonely clump of colored people who tend the boiling, this should be treated as a ceremony. This is worthy of something more than an isolated group of stirrers.

I continued to think this as I wandered over the country and came upon little mills dotted about in unexpected places. There was the superior mill in Georgia, a motor replacing the team of mules I had watched in Tennessee; an especially broken-down mill in North Carolina was tended by a family of poor whites, and the creak of the sweep and the sight of blue smoke rising in the air drew me down an impossibly rutty lane to a pathetic little gathering of syrup makers. It was quite a long time later that I discovered sorghum making to be really used as the basis for a ceremony. In the hills of southwest Virginia I was invited one day to a "'lasses boilin'." Now, at last I shall see what I seek, I decided as we drove off to the only folk social of their year. And there, in all its moving simplicity, it was completely right. To the tune of a fiddle, against the scent of wood smoke and the blue mist of the evaporating juice, we danced our square dances, dominated by the thick, sticky sweet smell of sorghum. The gentle rounded mountains were our setting, the sinking sun our illumination. As the sun disappeared from sight and night covered the skies, the fire from under the "boilin'" tossed shadows behind us, till there were two sets of dancers, we of the 'lasses boilin' and a strange black company of giants who footed it behind us, copying each step with maddening exactitude.

But the high point of the ceremony approached. Like participants at a sacrament, we drew near. This year's sorghum, essence of sun and rain and light and earth, was poured, hot still from the evaporators, upon biscuits. We ate, and tongues were burned by the heated syrup. But over everything, man and woman and child, and stretching black shadow, hung this sacramental feeling, like a mist of holiness. For deep in the heart of man, though he may live in an age of civilization that can build cities like New York and Chicago, San Francisco and Los Angeles, deep within him lies the need to celebrate and to worship, uncurbed and undestroyed by the machine. Here in the mountains of Virginia, with biscuit and sorghum, we held our little saturnalia; but simple though it might be, with a squeaky fiddle for music and smoke from evaporating syrup for incense, it held within this cup of the hills the spirit of all celebration and all earth worship. In the mountains of Virginia, on a night of October, sanity reigned unconquered.

PO' WHITE

HE WAS gathering pole beans when I first saw him, beans twined around the shabby buff stalks of the summer's stripped corn. I wondered why I had stopped in my walk along the road, for he was an ordinary-looking man in his faded blue overalls and peaked cap. I think it was a happy dignity in his movements that had made me pause, and he must have felt my interest in him, for he called to me. His voice had the same happiness that there was in his movements.

"I'm glad you've stopped," he shouted. "Hit's my birthday today, and I wanted to talk to someone. You've got to come and hear the quail callin' among my black-eyed peas between the corn. You've got to come and help me plow the sweet potatoes. You must watch while I strip the sorghum cane."

I looked straight into the face of this man who dared to command a complete stranger. It was a weather-burnt face, a face with fine bony structure and childlike eyes that were the blue of chicory flowers. It was a face that spoke of a sturdy heritage; and yet somewhere—exactly where, I could not say—somewhere there were signs of weakness and deterioration, as though the stock had reached its apex before this man's birth and was rushing rapidly downhill.

"It's about a snake that I stopped and wanted to talk to you," I called across to him. "There's one just back there, a few yards up the road, that's been

93

crushed by a car, and I was wondering whether you could tell me what it was."

He removed the corncob pipe from his mouth, where the stem had fitted into the gap of a lost front tooth.

"A snake?" he asked. "Why, there's not much as I don't know of snakes hereabouts. There's the spreadin' adder that changes color and spreads out flat when hit is attacked. There's the coachwhip snake who chases you and slashes at you with its knotted tail. There's the chicken snake and the rattler—but you don't need to mind about all those snakes. Why, my baby boy was sittin' on one the whole day long when he came out to watch his pappy plow, and I never did know hit till I went to give him a drink of water."

He had come nearer to me as he talked, measuring the lengths of the many snakes by the shifting of space between his two hands. Now he picked up the basket of beans that he had dumped upon the ground and joined me on the roadway.

"You'd best come and see my hogs," he told me. "They're in the fattenin' pen in the woods, just down past my home. They weigh already eight hundred pounds each and are so fat that they sits down to eat. Hit's a long time as I haven't seen better hogs, and hit won't be overlong now befo' the hog killin'. Mine's goin' dead at the November full moon; you don't lose no meat then as you do in December or January, when the weather's damper."

He lingered on the road and pointed across to our left.

"You see that house up there, up among the trees? That's my home. Hit don't look big, but hit's my home right enough. My grandpap he used to own all this land around here as far as your eye could see and further—way back past those first mountings and the cove to the next one, as far as where the sun goes down at night. But my grandpap he got a sort of wildness in him. I remember when I was a baby boy hearin' my pappy cussin' because his dad had gone and swapped three hundred acres of land for a double-barreled gun."

94

"So that's it," I thought. "That's where it began—the weakness that shows in his face."

But I had no time to reflect; he was going on talking.

"And then, since then, something seemed to have got into our blood and we couldn't keep hold of no land nohow. We just took to settin' on the porch and watchin' the land go to the bad. And it's poor land at that, and sour, so that the crawfish are comin' up through hit all over the place."

From where we stood I could see the house he had pointed out to me. It was a tumble-down structure, of the dogtrot pattern. Sacks flapped across the doors; old quilts were stuffed into broken windows.

A typical po' white, people would call him, I told myself. Po' buckra, white trash. And according to their standards they wouldn't be far wrong. I looked at his slouching, shambling walk, the boniness of his body, the weakness of his face. Yes, I decided. He's one of them. He's been driven back into the poor lands, and the urge to fight has died out in him. But how lovable he is, and how gentle.

Even while I was thinking this, he was beating aside the rough grasses that I might pass to the hogpen, beating down the summer cedar with the gentleness of a woman.

"Child," he was calling me, "I wouldn't have brought you through all this if I'd have known. Lordy, if I'd have known you was comin' today I'd have mowed hit down to make a path for you."

He knelt beside me, pulling off the beggar lice from my legs. He was a figure of great tenderness as he bent down in his old blue overalls.

I do not know how long it was that we sat by the fattening pen in the woods, among the goldening oaks. I only know that the Alabama sun crossed the sky and the shadows of the great trees shifted, till first the man's face and then his legs, and then my own head and then my body were warmed by the rays of the sun and then cooled by the shade of the tree trunks. I only know that the po' white beside

95

me leaned with abandon against one of these tree trunks as he poured out his thoughts on life.

It was sweet there on the earth near the hogpen, with the grass-hopper plow lying unused by the edge of the red pepper bushes, and the questioning form of Kate the mule looking round at us. It was sweet to feel outside of time and the rush of the world. It was good to listen to this man's voice.

Above us in the leaves a wren sang. A green grass snake slid through the undergrowth at our feet. Before us, in the fattening pen, his hogs grunted and squealed. But Jesse Perrick—for that, he told me, was his name—seemed to have the power to open his bony arms and gather to himself in friendship all living things, whether it were grass snake or wren, fattened hog, unknown woman or waiting mule. I looked up at him as he sat beside me, and there was a gentleness in his eyes that it was good to see. And as I looked at him, while he chewed tobacco and smiled towards his hogs, it seemed to me that quite lately I had seen that same look in the face of someone else. Oh, but not only once, I told myself. It's many, many times that you've seen it. It's in the face of the man who lives closely with animals. As you sat in the arena of the ram auction at Lynchburg and looked around you at the Virginian farmers you noticed that same childlike look in their eyes. And Charlie Rollins, near Shipman —surely you remember Charlie Rollins?

For a short while I forgot that it was Jesse Perrick who sat by my side under the oaks in Alabama. I was back in a little orchard in Virginia, where a sweet-faced man called, "Co—sheepy, co—sheepy, co—sheepy," and yoes and lambs and rams came running to him among the apple trees for the sprinkled piles of salt. Sweet was the face of the short, fair shepherd, sweet was the scene before me, of sloping orchard and pasture and a great blue wall of mountains beyond. The lilt of his call was answered by the tinkle of sheep bells. The shepherd was brushed by his close-clustering flock.

"And how is it that your sheep are so friendly?" I had asked him. "How is it that they are not afraid?"

His face had lit up in a lyrical smile.

"Why," he had said, "it's because no dog has ever frightened them. And if they've never been frightened, why, of course they're friendly and loving. That's just like life."

He had talked more, then, about life.

"It's what you've found out yourself that matters, and is truth," he had said firmly. "It isn't what you read in books. And I'll tell you what—it isn't things like dollars that bring you happiness. No, I tell you, it isn't."

The sheep bells tinkled beneath the apple trees. The lambs skipped among their dams.

But Charlie Rollins' voice sounded closer now. Why was it that he spoke about tobacco and not sheep? Or was it Charlie Rollins? I turned my head and saw my new friend Jesse Perrick smiling down at me.

"You've been silent for so long that I almost started to think that I had somehow vexed you. And I began to wonder what it might be. If my chewin' this tobacco isn't right pleasin' to you, why then I'll jest spit hit out."

He spat the strong, raisin-smelling tobacco from his mouth and wiped the stains from his face with the sleeve of his shirt.

"That be easy enough to do for you," he said. "Hit isn't the tobacco that's my enemy. It's liquor. I give it up for weeks at a time, but the devil of hit gets at me again and I'm as bad as ever befo'. Why, only the other day, I comes in so drunk that my old woman she chains me up and when I resists her she ups and takes an axe to me; and then of course I takes a gun to her. Hit's a powerful enemy, hit is, the liquor."

He had got up from my side, and was pulling me to my feet.

"You come with me. You come across to the end of this field, and I'll cut some sorghum cane for you to chew. If I peels a piece of sorghum cane for you, maybe you won't mind if I chews my tobacco."

Kate the mule had watched our movements. She whinnied now, and dragged at her chain.

"Whoa there, Kate," he called. "We ain't goin' plowin' potatoes no mo' today. You kin jest stand there and wait."

He turned to me.

"She's a right grand person, is Kate," he said. "And she knows everything I says. But she done cost me all of twenty-five dollars and I had to work a week or two in the city over there, in Montgomery, to buy her. And she hasn't earned her way yet."

He stroked her as he untangled the traces of the plow, and the same warm look came into his eyes that I had seen when he had pulled beggar lice from my bare legs.

How gentle he is, I thought. He wouldn't hurt a fly or an ant. I suppose people could call this man a failure; but they have such need of his tenderness and his love.

"Look at her," he was saying. "Look at the sweet expression she has in her eyes. We're powerful friends, Kate and me. And we have to be, for we're both of us lonesome. My family, you see, my family hit don't have no respect for me. Take my little uns. Why, the biggest've gone to the city already. 'None of this good-fer-nothin' life in the country for us, pappy,' they says. And the worst of hit is they've gone and turned my old woman from me, till there hain't nary soul in the home that loves me. You can believe me or not when I tell you that sometimes I sits silent in the evenin's for five or six days on end, and my old woman she don't open her mouth to me. They despises me, they do. And then of course, as I can't take no warm gentle woman to bed these days I takes my bottle of corn liquor. But hit isn't nothin' near so good."

He had cut some sorghum cane and was peeling it for me.

"Take that and chew it," he ordered me. "Hit's a day to celebrate. For hit's a day when I've got somebody to talk to—to talk to about the real things, like my sweet potatoes and my hogs. When a man goes around day after day, week after week, with nobody to look at things with, a happenin' like this is a miracle from the Lord God— and on my birthday, too."

Slowly we had wandered back to the highroad. As we neared his cabin, he seemed to hesitate.

"Hit isn't that I be ashamed of it," he said. "But you did ought to have knowed me one time years back, when I was earnin' fifteen to twenty dollars a day. That was when I left home and workin' in a sawmill, and befo' I married Melie. That was in the days of—"

A frightened look had come into this gentle face.

99

"How lovely the mountains look over there, in the north," I said, thinking to relieve the sudden tension. "It is just as though they skip and dance. Do you know the hill country well? Have you ever lived there?"

The frightened look deepened upon his face. He spoke now with a slow stammer.

"I lived there in them thar mountings some few years, I did. I lived thar after I left the sawmill, in the days when I were earnin' fifteen to twenty dollars a day."

A silence fell between us.

But I had understood.

Doesn't he trust me yet that much? I thought. Can't he see that I'd think no less of him?

A thin tired woman came across the path above us, carrying a baby before her in her arms. Her steps dragged as she walked. Her straw-colored hair lay in straggling wisps upon her shoulders.

"That's Melie. That's my old woman," said Jesse. "You mustn't mind her. She's po'ly these days. She's always po'ly, she is."

The woman turned her head as she saw us coming towards her. I could see her face more clearly now. It was the face of a worn-out creature, but in actual years it was still quite young. It was the figure of a woman exhausted by constant childbirth. Looking at her, I wondered how at her age she could have children who were old enough to have left home for the city, and wondering this I saw the life that lay behind her. Three little boys and a young girl played among the rocks at the side of the cabin. Lines of torn washing stretched from tree to tree. Among our feet strayed countless cats and dogs, chickens and ducks.

"Yes, this is my home," said Jesse. "All these livin' things . . . Come along here and talk to us, Stevie," he called to the nearest of the three little boys, who had stopped his playing to look our way.

But the child ran from us, to hide beneath some rocks.

"I'm crazy about them boys, but hit's their mother what has done it," he explained to me. "Hit's their mother and the two eldest what've gone to the city. They're ashamed of me and they're turnin' them all against me, till I'll be havin' nobody a-tall but Kate and my corn liquor. . . . But come with me. Come and see my tobacco patch, and we'll go on talkin'."

I followed him, though I had wanted to talk to Melie. But the woman had disappeared into the darkness of the cabin. I followed him past the cowshed and the disused smokehouse. I followed until we reached a sheltered patch of tobacco. The evening sun threw a long shadow from each plant, and our own shadows, as we stood by the patch, rippled across many rows.

"We might as well worm them," said Jesse. "We might jest as well worm them while we talk—for they should 'a' been done and cut long time back."

Searching the great full leaves for the fat green tobacco worm, stamping the juicy, leaf-fed worms underfoot, we talked. We talked of the earth of Alabama, of the grasses and the weeds, the pests and the harvests. As time went on our talk turned to the mountains that danced and leapt away to the north. Here in the seclusion of the tobacco patch, I felt, here among the leaves and the worms and the earth, here I might learn the secret of his fear.

He drew a bottle of corn liquor from his pocket and handed it to me.

The fierce liquor burned my throat. I gave him the bottle back.

"This ain't near so good as what I did use to make," he said, tipping the bottle into his open mouth. "This is right poor stuff. What I made, why, hit was known for miles around, hit was. Hit was a mixture of corn and rye, and there was folks in the city what knew that no one could equal Jesse Perrick's moonshine—though they didn't exactly know it was me what made it. Five dollars a gallon, hit was, and a whole month in a charcoal-lined keg before hit was ever sold. And none of those newfangled things added to hit as you'd find in this stuff we're drinkin' now. There was Government people and revenooers what was drinkin' it by the gallon and never knowin' where the copper still was in them mountings where it came from. I was makin' fifteen to twenty dollars a day, I was, in them times of prohibition."

Again he handed me the corn liquor, and when I shook my head he emptied the bottle down his own throat. We sat at the edge of the tobacco patch, and the mountains grew lilac in the evening light.

"Nobody didn't know where Jesse Perrick's still was, for he laid a pipe within a hollow tree trunk so that the smoke came out into the sky high up among the tops of the big trees. Nobody, so I thought, didn't even know that I was makin' moonshine, and the dollars rolled in each day. None of that small business for Jesse Perrick. I took my liquor to Montgomery and Birmingham, where it was drunk by the big city folks. . . . If you can move a little nearer this way—there, that's hit, just a little nearer—you can see that great mass of trees on those mountings just to the right, from where we're sittin', just to the right of the tip of that last tobacco plant on the far row. No," he said as he drew me yet farther to his side, "not where you're lookin'. Further to the right yet."

The mountains seemed to me a blurred wall of lilac. But to please him I pretended to see the great mass of trees he pointed to.

"Well, follow that path through them trees, and bend then to the left, past a small clearin' where I raised corn, and an old shack where nobody hain't ever lived since I was a boy. There's a big tangle of brushwood and undergrowth lies straight befo' you, but you must get around that and wind your way among the oaks and the sour-wood trees till it would seem like you was lost. I didn't suppose nobody but Jesse Perrick ever went thar. I was livin' alone in them days, I was, in a one-roomed cabin near a little branch. And there, past the cabin, in the very middle of the thick trees, I had my still. And the birds was my friends, and the squirrels and the rattlers. And as hit did turn out, hit were a good thing I'd gotten used to livin' alone, for that made my seven years in jail seem more natural like, with nobody to talk to."

"But what happened?" I asked him, as he paused. "Did the revenue men give you as much as seven years when they found you?"

"No, hit warn't exackly that. Hit warn't a revenooer what made that cracklin' noise in the undergrowth that mornin' in September.

I remember it, as clear as if hit had happened yesterday, for there weren't never no sounds like that around me. I stopped in what I were doin', and stood straight and still; for I knew hit were a man comin'. 'They've caught you at last,' I says to myself. 'Jesse Perrick, they've caught you at last.' And then I tells myself that sooner or later this happens to every moonshiner as ever made liquor. And I prepares to give myself up, for the sound of the man was so near that there weren't no ghost of a chance for me to run away. And then the man appears before me. And he ain't no revenooer after all, but an ornery man with a gun. And I knows as he has come to steal my still. And befo' I can think what to do, the man calls to me in a husky whisper, 'Get the hell out of here, or I'll shoot,' and I'd have been a dead un if he hadn't 've tripped in the brush, so as I had time to whip round and get my own gun from the side of the door. 'Hit's him or me,' I tells myself, and I shoots. And the great body falls in a heap among the bushes, and hit seemed like I shot well. But the mountings betrayed me, for they tossed the sound of that shot about like a ball they was playin' with."

He leaned forward to remove a tobacco worm from the leaf of a plant that brushed his shoulder.

"Hit's a mighty purty thing, a tobacco worm is," he murmured. "All green with them thin lines of black and white on hit. Hit be so right purty that hit do seem all wrong to kill it."

Gently he placed the worm back, that it might feast upon the leaf.

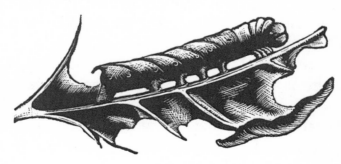

MOUNTAINS

S THE WORLD shook around me, it seemed that never had there been more need for some one thing that was beyond alteration. Bombs wiped out cities, "scorched earth" blackened stretches of the world's map, and all that we had held enduring melted before the eyes like snow in a shaft of sun. It was as though we hurtled across the surface of a maelstrom, and nowhere could we find unity or changelessness. If this alteration were the force of growth, I felt, it would be in harmony with instinct; for as the child grows to the man, and the seed to the towering plant, so there is ever change. But here was the changing force of destruction. I sought security. There above me in the night skies Orion and the Pleiades and all the pale stars went their ordered way, and the sun rose each day, crossed the heavens, and set, though armies fell. But the heavens with their stars were remote and unsatisfying. I needed something closer, something that I could encompass with my finite understanding. Even if it were but for a little space of time, I felt, I should have gained strength enough to cope with this mad world.

It was in this state of mind that I looked westward to the mountains. With a rush of Biblical faith I knew that it was from them that salvation would come. "The mountains and the hills shall break forth before you into singing . . ." Yes, but what was the beginning of that verse? "For ye shall go out with joy, and be led forth with peace."

Over many years we can read something, and with our eyes and our lips and our brains we follow the words; but as Paul's revelation came to him unheralded, so we can never know at what exact moment words we read may flame into meaning.

"The mountains and the hills shall break forth before you into singing." As my car crossed the quivering heat of North Carolina I knew that I went the road to Damascus.

The rivers rise and fall, I told myself; the trees grow and are cut down; harvests alter the color and picture of the earth around me; the child grows to the man. Mountains alone are absolute in their unchangingness. And as I approached these mountains, that are the oldest in existence, though I had never before seen them I felt that in coming to them I was coming home.

I wondered why I was feeling this, knowing myself to be so completely a stranger here. And then I understood what was happening to me. Some strange sense outside factual proving told me that I was returning to my own people.

Maybe you're just a century or two late, I reflected; but, all the same, they are your own people.

And suddenly I knew that objective time matters little, and that there must be deep race memories beyond all understanding. And, knowing this, I saw myself again as a young girl stand bewitched on the heather-covered moors of Scotland as I first heard the sound of bagpipes. Something beyond the findings of science stirred in my blood and I became, back across the centuries, the Jacobite of the days of my forebears.

So, now, I knew within me that I was returning to my people.

These are your own, some sense in my blood told me, these who speak the language of your ancestors, and dance as your forebears danced, and sing the songs that echoed across the Highland glens when your clans fought for Bonnie Prince Charlie. You are just a little late in coming; but that is all.

And then it happened; it happened not, as some would choose to think, as a coincidence or a miracle. It happened as one of those moments of reality that are our due. I stopped at a turn on the mountain road by a small cabin. I stopped, for I had heard, above the noise of my car, a plaintive sound. Woven into this plaintive sound was a man's singing. I knew this song. I had known it before I was born. I looked up at the porch of the cabin and there, at the far end, I saw the singer. He was a mountain man, gaunt and loose-limbed. He sat on a wooden stool, and upon his knee lay a gracious-shaped dulcimer which he picked with a goose quill and a cane reed. His tiny child was at his feet, rocking in rhythm. And he was singing the ballad of "Barbara Allen." As I listened to him, I knew the indestructibility of the human spirit. This man, picking his dulcimer and singing this ballad, stood for the pathos of transplanting. Here in this one human creature was all the unconscious homesickness of the world. I knew that what we bring with us to a new country as of greatest worth is our songs, and the sense of unbroken continuity of the spirit of man seemed to me a thing of moving beauty.

But what was he singing now? I listened and heard yet another ballad. This time it was "The Wife of Usher's Well." Songs that had long since been forgotten in the land of their creation endured here among these immutable hills of North Carolina that, with their own haunting eternity, had the power to guard unchanged a people and its lore.

He had not seen the country that gave birth to these ballads, this mountain man sitting on his porch: he did not know it with the mind and with the brain. But I like to suppose that somewhere within his blood a race memory stirred that was beyond reasoning.

For as I listened to his singing, something very strange was happening to me: I was being swept by an emotion that I found hard to explain. It was the emotion of homesickness, and it was not for the England I had left, but for a people and a country I had never seen.

As I felt this I was filled with complete understanding, for the first time, of the nostalgia that took the American to Europe. I heard again the voice of a New York man, suddenly unrecognizable, almost, in its deep feeling as he told me of his pilgrimage to Scotland. I remembered how his voice had trembled—this controlled, hardened city man—as he recalled the moment he first stepped upon Scottish soil. "Something came over me," he had said, "and without knowing what I was doing I knelt and kissed that earth, for I knew I belonged. And as it were in a telescoped moment of time, so I felt within me my entire past, back before my birth, and knew that never could the streets of New York be to me what the earth of Scotland was." And so, too, into this whining pattern of sound of the picked dulcimer, was woven the story of the old pink-faced man from the Middle West whom I had met years ago in a graveyard in Cornwall. For a long while I had watched this bent figure as it wandered from tombstone to tombstone, and with the intolerance of a husky young Englishwoman I had laughed within me at the sentimentality of the old American. He had tears in his eyes that sparkled in the sun as he turned my way, and I had felt shame at being witness to this weakness. But he was not ashamed, and there was a glow upon his face and a triumph in his voice as he talked to me. "I've worked hard all my days," he said, "all my days, since early childhood I have worked that I might get enough money to come back here, to this graveyard, as I have done today. For these are my people, and this is my earth, and it is here that I belong." Courteously I listened, and courteously I showed him around the village. But it was with a lifeless spirit that I did it, and a heart that had no understanding. Secure upon my own earth, in the land of my mother's forebears, I knew nothing of the power of nostalgia; this old man with the tearful eyes was but one more American tourist.

And now, in these mountains of North Carolina, I was conscious of the strangest two-way emotion. Here was I, a Scottish, Cornish woman, a European, swept by nostalgia for this new country of America. Here was I overpowered by race memory as I listened to a ballad that had been lost to my own people amidst the confusion of empire expansion and the distortion of the machine age. I sat at the wheel of my car, unwilling to move, as I understood the power of nostalgia. Never again could I smile at an old American who had crossed the seas to seek his ancestors. It was my turn now to make a pilgrimage of homage. Though it were to a people who had left my land in the days of Culloden, yet I knew that something within me would recognize my kin. If anything worried me, it was lest I should be considered the alien stranger. I sought a password, that I might be known to belong.

While I was living this lifetime of emotion the sun was sinking low behind the mountains, throwing long slate-blue shadows down their flanks. The buff of the dead cornstalks upon the upright fields was warmed by the sunset, and the sky, a pale turquoise-blue, was whipped with orange scarves of clouds. Before me lay seven mountain ranges, pink, violet, grey, blue, melodramatic as the back scene of an opera. Soon, I knew, abrupt darkness would fall. I had far to go, but the mountain man on the porch was singing still to his dulcimer, and the serenity of this world about me, these tree-clad, rounded mountains that seemed to draw my hand towards them, that they might be stroked, mingled with the Riddle Song from "Captain Stafford's Courtship" that rose now into the air, straight and gentle, like smoke from a cabin chimney; and the magic of this world held me till I sat and waited, while the sun sank and the evening star showed in the sky.

"I gave my love a baby, there's no cryen' . . . "

The sweetness of the Riddle Song followed me as I drove up the first mountain and down across the little cove at the other side. The words threaded themselves into the purr of my car, till I seemed, with the car, to become the song and the mountains and the people who sang.

"A cherry when hit's bloomin', hit has no stone . . ."

On and on this song went in my mind, until it blurred into the plaintive tune of "Cotton-Eyed Joe" and the "Cherry Tree Carol." They overlaid one another, the songs I had just heard, and I was song-drunk as I drove over the mountains in the hastening dusk. On the porches of lonely cabins that I passed sat white-dressed women,

looking like great moths or white flowers in a garden at night. Even from the isolation of my car I could feel their serenity as they sat there quietly, without fret, gazing over the great mountains before them while they rested from their work.

I can't stand it, all this beauty, I felt. Now, here, so suddenly to be surrounded by sanity, it is too much. It seemed to me that I must waken at any moment from this peace and rightness to the world of war. Here around me I was aware of a strong simple pattern of life, a primal pattern that concerned itself only with essentials. Here, I knew I would mingle with a people who lived at the dictates of its blood and its instincts, unconfused by the modern world. And they go and call these people quaint and old-worldly, and would make them self-conscious, I told myself. While all the time these mountain folk have merely kept a hold on the enduring values of life.

Though it was nearing night and all that I had seen of the people was one mountain singer on his porch and some tired women resting in the dusk, yet already the spirit of the mountains had begun to work its enchantment upon me and I knew that I was in an unbelievable world of sanity.

Weeks of enchantment followed, weeks of such enrichment of spirit as, in this tortured world of today, one had almost forgotten could exist. And their enrichment lay in their sanity, this same sanity that I had felt the first evening at dusk as I drove over the mountains. Here was a people with a philosophy that was invulnerable. If only this way of living could be followed, I found myself thinking so often, there need be no wars. Joe Wallis sat beside me on the porch of his cabin at sundown, looking over the stretching coves and distant mountains, and as we drank glass after glass of the cider we had made together that afternoon from the windfall Virginia Wonders that covered the ground by the springhouse, he began to tell me of his content. "We don't somehow need much money," he said. "We can grow almost all we needs—so what would we be doing with money?" I looked about me at the apple trees that crept up his hillside, at the cow that grazed in the meadow, at the beehives in his garden. His crib was piled with corn, and his yard with cordwood. Within the cabin his tall, wide-hipped wife canned the vegetables of her raising. Even the tobacco in Joe Wallis's pipe came from the small slanting field behind the smokehouse, and rumor had it that somewhere in the bottom of the cove, hidden among the brush, the shucked corn that had started to sprout in the darkness of the sacks at the back of the farthest shed was made into mash. We ate peanut butter biscuits, and chinquapins, and grapes from the vines in the garden patch, and as I followed his gaze I began to feel that I knew something of what was so wrong with the world. It's that we haven't known how to cope with civilization, I decided. We've lost trace of the main pattern of living and have denied our instincts. And I looked around at my companion and saw that the content in his face was the result of self-respect, and that this self-respect came solely from the fact that he lived a normally creative life. Here was none of the thwarted, dulled look that we find upon the face of the assembly line worker. This uneducated mountain man had a live concern for growth and work and lived in harmony with his earth. "They've been threshing way out at Ed Bolder's today," he said now, gazing far off into space. "I can see the strawstacks. Look, way back there past the second cove, to the left." I followed his eyes, but I was not so good at reading the language of the book of the earth as this man by my side. We drank glass after glass of the newly made cider, and he laughed as he told me of the "voluntary" apples that grew on his hillside. "Why," he said, "I did use to go for so many walks up there, whilst eating apples, and did throw away so many cores with the seeds, that the trees have grown." I looked at my Johnny Apple-seed of the mountains, and knew that civilization was not able to give him anything that he needed.

His wife came out from the cabin and joined us on the porch. She had the dark, deep-set eyes of the mountain woman, and her brown bony arms brushed back the white hair smoothly from her forehead as she settled herself on the wooden bench beside us. I looked at the bushy black brows, the long serene sweet face, and I felt that she was as gentle as these hills, but as inscrutable.

"In the common manner the frost and cold weather comes with the new moon," she said suddenly, in her slow voice. "So we should have our first frost this Saturday. And to think of all the vegetables still out there in the yard." She sighed, but as she turned to the view before her a light came into her grave eyes. "It puzzles me how any-one should ever want to go away anywhere from here, it's so beauti-ful in these mountains."

We sat there quietly and without speaking, and as I watched my companions it seemed to me that I was watching complete repose. It was the same repose that I had found in all these mountain people. The evening before, in the soft lamplight of Rob Stewart's cabin, I had studied the simple strong planes of his face, accented by the lamp. Against the shadows the man sat heavily in his chair, and arms and folded hands and long legs rested with abandon. Here in this figure before me was no conflict. The body sank to rest with the same weight that we feel in a hound that sleeps after a day of hunting. There was an animal beauty in the man, and an animal gentleness. Into the night we sat there, and the oil lamp threw lights and shadows that were as simple as the man sitting in the chair. It sparkled on the buttons of his denim coat and picked out the metal on the banjo that hung against the wall. And as I listened to the ha'nt tales this man was telling me, the shadows that the lamp threw into the room took on the form of the lady in the check cotton dress and the abundant black hair, who would come each night and feel along the mantel-piece from one end to the other, as though she were looking for something; and the man seated in the chair would seem to shrink till he was the little boy who had seen the ha'nt, burying his head beneath the bedclothes in terror, lest he should cry out and show his fear. Or the darkness of the room would change and become the darkness among the laurels on the top of the knob, where the bushes are so thick that even in the daytime you can hardly see your way. We wait for the laurel spectre that nobody has ever seen. "You hear the strangest things there, and there just isn't any place where a horse or a mule or any such could ride. But sure as life, if'n you're there and you stand still you hear the greatest sound of a wild riding of something that passes along near you towards the branch, and the laurel bushes are stirred and you can hear hoofs. You can't never see nothing, not I can't. But I did once come across someone—Jim Boone, it were—what did see something. He were up thar with his mule and he couldn't see nothin'; but that mule, she did, for she bucks and shrinks close against the fur edge of the laurels and won't budge for nobody and brays as if she be fur scared. Jim didn't see no animal pass, but he sure heard the same wild rushing ride of something. And then as the mule shrinks back against the laurels, he looks down toward where the mule has drawn away from, and thar he sees what looks like a calf hide all spread out upon the ground. That war all, for he jest rode away as hard as he could, as scared as his mule."

From out of his tranquility Rob Stewart can conjure up ha'nts that could terrify the most unimaginative of people. He sits in his chair striking matches upon the metal of his coat buttons as he lights his wild-rose-wood pipe. The light from the match, against his face, shows me the happy, good look in his eyes and the sweetness of his smile. I had noticed the same smile earlier that day in his grown daughter, as I helped her prepare roasting corn for pickle, scraping it off the ear with a knife, till the juice spattered our shoes and our dresses. I had seen it even in the face of his sick wife as she lay in bed and told me she couldn't pick the banjo any more; pain could not take the sweetness from her face.

Rob Stewart was not able to cure her. His father had been a "conjure" and by rights he, too, could have been one; for he was also the seventh son of the seventh son. But Rob was afraid of this power, for his father had said that in the end every "conjure" dies of one of the sicknesses he has cured. And he was sure of it—as sure of it as he was that his father had cured cancers all over the place. And he would tell me then how he had noticed that when his father was curing someone he would go out in the morning bright and early, before speaking to a soul, and stroke or touch the branch of a certain cedar tree, and the limb would die as the disease got well.

Here in the isolation of these mountains, shut off from the dilution of civilization, there is such intensity of living and thinking and feeling that any extension beyond the ordinary limits of human experience is easily believed. Spectre weavers return to their earthly looms in the dead of night, and a tale is told of a spinning wheel that, should you wake at midnight, you would find moved to the center

of the room, only to be back in its accustomed place next day. But these people, uncomplicated by city life, are capable of such deep love for their homes and their work tools that, were it a possibility, surely they of all people would return after death.

As I walked home along the black lanes, as I crossed the rushing little river on the wooden swinging bridge and groped my way up the winding mountain road, strange shapes of ghosts and witches lined my path. An apple fell to the ground with a loud thud, and I jumped nearly into the ditch. The wooden swinging bridge creaked in the night breeze, and I thought of the wagon and team that went off into a place and were never seen again. A cow mooed in a field as I passed, and my mind went back to Rob Stewart's tale of the cow that was bewitched. "And so they went to a witch doctor about it and he told them to strip the cow down nine times into a frying pan, to put this over the fire and stab it with a knife until all the milk had boiled and burnt away. Nine days from then the cow would be all right." I could hear his soft voice in the oil-lit room and could see the smoke from his pipe curl into the air. The world around me tonight was filled with limitless possibilities. But I was not really scared, for above me and surrounding me was the guardianship of these gentle hills, and in my mind I could see the serene peace upon the faces of the mountain people.

There was little possibility to feel eerie next day, with the mountain sides heavy with dew and a fling of morning-glories over the ditches; pink, blue, purple, white, white with five blue strokes, white with pink stripes, crimson, they were the colors of the wash dresses of young girls, as they bloomed among the green-yellow of the budding goldenrod. Apple trees studded with crimson fruit looked bright against the scarves of white mist that lay, still, across the mountains, like sudden lakes above which the mountaintops emerged, as in a Japanese print.

I walked quickly along the narrow path that runs round the foot of the knob, for there was a bite in the air. As I walked I smelt the good scent of wood smoke, and suddenly as I turned a corner of the path I knew where it came from. A woman in a pink dress stirred a great black kettle over a wood fire. Into the scent of the wood smoke was blended the sweet scent of apples being cooked. She was making apple butter. The coolness of the morning pulled me toward the heat of the fire, and as I drew nearer I could see this woman. Tall, as all these mountain people are, she had the dark deep-set eyes of Mrs. Wallis, and with her Roman nose and black hair drawn back to a little bun at the nape of her neck, she looked like a foreign beauty, or almost as though she had Indian blood in her. But where did these intensely dark-eyed women come from, I wondered. There seemed to be nothing of the Anglo-Saxon about them, and as this woman in pink turned toward me and smiled there was a scriptural beauty in her face. So, I felt, should Rachel have looked, or Ruth. And then I thought of the women of Wales and of Scotland, the dark-haired Celts, and I recognized my kin.

The apple butter has come to the boil now and bubbles like great round muddy volcanoes. The woman keeps the wooden stirrer in motion, that the mixture may not burn. But as the butter boils with more vigor it splashes over onto our legs and gets redder and stickier. At the far side of the great black kettle stands a little girl, pouring the uncooked liquid into the bubbling mass. The wind blows the smoke into our eyes, and would lay the fire level if it were not for two pieces of old tin that have been erected as a guard. "Hit's a good run of apple butter," the woman calls to me above the crackling of the wood fire. And her face is lighted by a smile. Behind her stretches an orchard that slopes up towards the knob. Mountains surround us. Once again I am filled with wonder at the beauty of this world about me, and fear lest at any moment I waken and find it to be a dream.

And so they crowd upon me, these memories, and I see an aged quilt maker—as old, she seemed, as the hills that billowed around her cabin. Her eyes were red and bleary, her face ravined in wrinkles.

Yet between sunup and sundown of one day she had quilted a crimson and yellow coverlet. Passing her open door at midday, I had stopped to watch her. The quilting frame, hanging by ropes from the low ceiling, occupied the whole of the room, and the old woman and one of her daughters bent low over their work. As I entered the cabin door she came to meet me, and though I was a complete stranger she held my hand strong and tight and stroked my arm while she smiled her toothless smile. "Child," she muttered, "if you're ever down Marion way you must come and see me. My name's Grindstaff. They'll know me. What's that? How many quilts have I made? I wouldn't be able to tell you how many I'd made in my life-time. No, child, I jest wouldn't." The bleary eyes looked into my face with such kindness, and the clasp of her hand grew even tighter. I left them, to climb the mountain, and when I returned, in early evening, the quilting was finished and the table was laid for three.

"You are so friendly," I stammered as I sat down. "You don't know me, but you are so friendly."

"But that's the sort of people I like to go among," said the daughter. "And that's the sort I like to have around me—people who are friendly. I always bring my children up to be friendly, because I never know where they'll be."

Everywhere I went in these mountains I found friendliness, and with this friendliness went trust and a belief in the goodness of all creatures. Thinking this, I remembered Nick Campbell, resting from his wood chopping on the laurel slope behind his home. "I don't see no reason why folks should shun one another," he had said, as he wiped the sweat from his ugly wide face, and spat tobacco. "I'm always friendly with a person till I finds I can't be—and that don't never really happen. . . . There, right down there is my plank where I feed my squirrels with walnuts. I loves them, and even the little squirrels know when a person is goin' to be kind to them. . . . Nobody's a stranger to me. I'd never seed a stranger."

These words haunted me, and still haunt me. But why should they be reserved for life among the mountains? I have asked myself this so many times. Why, when I think of them, must my mind go back to Nick Campbell? But I sit again beside the old man with the lovable ugliness, and listen as he swallows and gulps and spits. Perhaps he is chopping his wood, giving a strange rough little "huff" each time he lowers his axe, or pausing to explain why he can't work as hard as he used to, being now eighty-five years old. But the pauses are few, and the sound of the chopping continues for, he says, "I dreads the winter and I likes to get my wood and my feed in for the winter well befo' the mean weather comes. Hit were plum cold this morning, hit were, and hit weren't easy to get out of bed." As he chops, his figure dappled by sunlight, it isn't easy to see where he ends and the earth and the tree trunks begin, they seem to be so much of a oneness, and of the same color and the same substance. But he tires easily, and the voice that from time to time gets all squeaky goes on talking. "Hif I was able to find someone as could do my hard work I'd let him," he tells me. "But my son he says to me, 'Pappy, hif you was to come and live with me you wouldn't have to do no work whatever,' and I said to him, 'In that case I jest can't come, for I'd be dead hif'n I didn't work' . . . . But not that I wouldn't like to stop doing all this hard work." Once again he lifts the axe and the strange little "huff" sounds upon the air.

Or perhaps we are walking the mountain sides, as he shows me a view he loves, and because the sun is hot we sit in the shade of his old storehouse in the dell, where the sun cannot reach us. He picks up windfall apples for me and gives me spring water from a dipper. "This jest suits me, settin' here," he says; and he tells me how he bought this land, bit by bit, starting back in the days when he and his wife were young. "When I were a little boy my pappy rented this land, and I did use to play with the kids of the man who owned it and they would say to me, 'This hisn't your land but our pappy's'; and hit made me so mad that I set to work to buy little parcels of the land, till now I have enough for my eight children, and each share with good spring water and a road on it." Tale would overlap tale, till the sun had lost its heat and stood low in the sky. "Hit seems like the time slipped," Nick Campbell would say as we started for home. "I was enjoyin' myself, I reckon."

"I've never seed a stranger." As the words come back to me I watch serene-faced women weaving in the loneliness of remote coves, happy in the self-respect of creating. Or I am at a singin' at the Liberty Hill church, and the women nurse their babies while the fanatical preacher tells them of the glories of heaven. The screaming of the infants rivals the singing out of the books with the shaped notes. At the far side of the church sit the mountain men, their arms laid along the backs of the pews as they gaze out of the open window, where the wheat shocks can be seen marching over the hills. And when the singin' is over the people visit their dead in the tiny grave-yard at the back of the church, the women with their little sourwood toothbrushes in their mouths, for the dipping of the snuff, the young girls gay in their bright-colored dresses, like a garden of flowers. "That's Mr. Brasswell, that is," says Myrtle Hillier as she gazes softly down at one of the graves. "He do lie in a purty spot, he do." Friendliness extends beyond the grave, here in the mountains.

And so they surround me and protect me, these people of the earth: the mountain singer on the porch, Joe Wallis, Nick Campbell, Rob Stewart, the aged quilt maker, the weavers who live unafraid alone in the far-off coves. And as they surround me and fortify me with sanity in a tortured, diseased world I find they are joined by others. They are joined by kinsfolk who have never crossed the seas: Tom Grainger, the plowman from the farm in the Chiltern Hills, George Gaydew, the Devon woodman, Annie Beachey, the grave-digger from the Cornish village, the Scotch shepherd in the Highland glen. "Nobody's a stranger to me. I've never seed a stranger," said an old man of eighty-five in the mountains of North Carolina; and the echo of his words is tossed from land to land, defying frontier and language, overpowering army and enemy. For they are the words of a man who knows the brotherhood of the earth.

LOUISIANA PILGRIMAGE

IT'S SWEET, sitting here in the sun. The light upon the live oaks seems to turn the Spanish moss to smoke. I know exactly the shapes of the shadows as the day passes. I could trace the form of the trunk of that great oak over there if I were blindfolded. I know just where each knot and gnarl comes. I know where the lowest branches reach out to hold their moss and where the tender green leaves sprout in spring. It seems to me that each of those oaks has its memories of something we did when we were small. That one to the left, which forks into three great branches at about the height of a young boy's shoulders, that's the tree James and I used to climb; and little Martha would stand at the foot and cry out in fear. Yes, and Grandmamma would come along and scold us for frightening Martha. And that far oak with the branches that bend low to the ground almost—that's where I first kissed Maisie, there, hidden behind the long tresses of moss, where nobody could see us from the house. It's as though each tree kept its own secret with me. It's almost as though they were something more than trees. . . . And to think that strangers will pass by these trees. To think that they will stop and look at them and say, "Why, what perfectly beautiful live oaks," and walk on, and never know that it was something more than just trees that they looked at.

I wonder if old Sam is standing out at the main gates. I wonder if he'll remember to take his top hat off and bow as each car comes past. That was a grand idea Maisie had, to dress him up like that, in top hat and frock coat and all. She'd never have thought of it, Maisie wouldn't, if it hadn't been for young Sophie Bisland who knows the sort of thing that'll fetch the Yankees. Maisie has never spent her time thinking over what would pay. And those white whiskers of Sam's, there's a pathos about them that should touch the crowds. There's a strange sadness to a negro who grows old and whose hair turns white, even though Tom Jackson did have the cruelty to tell old Sam that he looked just like a Kodak negative, all black with his white hair and white whiskers. . . . Damn that young pup. He and his sort don't know old Sam. They don't know how he must hate all this. They weren't set on his knee when they were so tiny they could hardly toddle, while he told them tales of when he was a little one. They never sneaked off with him when nobody was looking and were carried over the levee and down through the sipe water to the river's edge, to stare at that great stretching Mis'sippi. They never listened to him as he sang "Somebody touched me" or "Hand me down the silver trumpet, Gabriel," feeling sure that the angel Gabriel would at any moment break through the clouds above our heads to obey the old negro. . . . And now all I do for him, now he's old and white-haired, is to stand him in the middle of the road like a pimp, to catch strangers.

Oh, Sam, do you forgive me? Do you hate what I'm doing with you? Do you hate it as much as I do?

I know what the Pilgrimage folks will say: "And were you a slave when you were young?" I've told him to say he was—one of the last slaves in this parish. That'll fetch them. It's the sort of thing they want, those Yankees. They fight to rid us of our slaves, and then they come all the way down to what they call the Deep South so that they can catch a glimpse of a real live nigger that was born in slavery. . . . Oh, Sam, we'd never have done it if we hadn't been driven. I swear by these live oaks I love so much, and by the moss and the azaleas and the Cherokee roses, I swear we'd never have done it if it hadn't been for the taxes and the cotton crop being so sorry and Bayard's college fees and all. I swear we'd never have let a soul come within these gates that wasn't a friend—no, least of all a Yankee. . . .

Perhaps nobody will come after all. Yes, perhaps nobody will come. And then I can turn to Maisie and say that I've done my best, and what more can I do? And we can bring Sam in and tell him he can sit in the sun by the back porch and look out upon the azaleas in bloom—yes, and take off those foolish clothes.

The sun is sweet just now, the end of March. How gentle and kind it is, with no thought for dollars. I could sit here by the hour. I could sit and watch the light shift among the moss and the oaks. I could sit and listen to that redbird over there by the sloping terraces. "De-ar—de-ar—de-ar," he sings. The sadness of his song seems to suit this place. It suits the gloom of the moss. It is one with the ghosts that creep around and stare at me with reproach in their eyes. They never leave me. They confront me. They dog my steps wherever I go, till I could scream and run and shout to them: "Take it, then. Take the whole damn place. Take it and protect it from the world of today. Only let me go free. Let me escape from the tangle of the moss and the enchantment of the birds' songs. Rid me of the sweet burden of the place, so that I may really live, even now, at my age, instead of existing among ghosts." But the ghosts weave around me a film of the past, and I am unable to escape.

Perhaps nobody will come. I think I really will tell Sam he can leave his post out there on the main highway and sit in the sun. Funny, even remembering Maisie and the girls, it's Sam that upsets me most. To think of exploiting that white hair of his is more than I can stand. Sam, do you really forgive me? Can you ever understand how it was forced upon me? You with your childlike faith, how can you see what's happening to the world? It's beyond you to comprehend that you and I and this place with its white columns and its magic have ceased to be a reality and have become a museum for the world to gaze at. The pulse has gone from our life. We're lost, you and I. We're lost in the past. We live backwards, and the world marches forward, to machinery and airplanes and speed. We—

What's that sound? Something is coming up the drive, way back there past the first clump of white azaleas. There's a car coming. Somebody is coming. . . . I can't face it. . . . I can't stand it. I'll go in and call Maisie. . . . I'll tell them it was all a mistake and that this

place isn't open to the public. I'll tell them they've been misinformed.

But it's too late. They're here. They're getting out. They're coming towards me. What was it Maisie told me? I must remember that Southern hospitality is one of the things these Yankees look for, just as much as the moss and the slaves and the white columns and the pralines. I must be gracious and warm. I must treat them as though they were my guests, each one of them, and as though it gave me pleasure to welcome them.

" . . . Yes, the house was built in 1829. No, ma'm, General Sherman didn't pass this way. What was that, ma'm? Yes, Sam was one of the few remaining slaves—that is, he was born in slavery but was freed when he was but a year or two old. His old wife, Mammie, is inside the house. You will see her when you go in. Won't you step along this way, ladies? Yes, fifty cents for each visitor, and a reduction if it's a large party. Not at all, ma'm, not at all. Delighted to have the honor of showing it to you."

That was done. Perhaps it wasn't so bad after all. And four of them makes two dollars. That's two dollars easily earned. . . . I wonder how Sam liked it. It looks as though he played his part well, for that fat lady with the Middle West accent was all worked up about how cute he was. Oh, Sam, try to enjoy it. Try to forgive me, if you can.

I wonder how Maisie is getting on. I hope she had time to mend that hole in the back of her crinoline. Lucky I saw it. Lucky I went behind her as she tripped down the stairs. If she'd lifted her arms high to point out the hand-carved woodwork she'd have split it further. It's getting old and shabby, that crinoline of Grandmamma's. But perhaps it looks more real that way. Only, Maisie hasn't got the slim, delicate, laced-in figure of Grandmamma. She can't carry it in the same way, and she looks as if she were in fancy dress. Or is that what she really looks like? Isn't it perhaps more true that she looks like a ghost—a ghost of herself? And the girls' dresses, too. They're all wrong. They're like a ghost, too, each one of them. Ghosts among ghosts among ghosts. And I'm a ghost, it would seem. I must not rebel, for it would spoil the atmosphere of the place, and the dollars would not roll in. It would get around. They would say this house wasn't worth visiting, wasn't real in spirit. It must be ghosts among ghosts, ghosts in a dwelling place for ghosts.

Listen. That's Maisie speaking. I had forgotten how soft and sweet her voice was, curly like the fronds of a fern in early spring. And that other voice, the harsh pointed one like an angry rooster, that must belong to the short woman in the grey tweeds. . . . What's that she's asking? A recipe for pickles? Pralines? Maisie, dear, dear Maisie, don't forget your part. Now's the moment for Mammie to appear—great fat soft sprawling Mammie, Mammie who held our babies close against her warm black body, Mammie who piled the blankets upon us all when we had the chills. . . . Yes, good Maisie. You've not forgotten. That's Mammie's voice now, as soft and sprawling as her great fat body. I can see how she stands there, all got up in her spotted bandanna, and the massive black arms crossed over the white apron. What's that? "Fust of all, ma'm, I sho' must have mo' pecans if I's to make mo' pralines. And there hain't no mo' pecans round here." . . . What's that the woman in the tweeds is saying?

She'll find out where more pecans can be bought. Doesn't she know we can't afford to buy them? Can't she understand? But no, she musn't. She musn't know how poor we are. She must think it's Southern hospitality in the grand manner that makes us open our home to her. That's it. The generous spirit of the times. The generous spirit that makes us show her into the bedroom where I brought Maisie on our marriage, where I undressed her and gazed at the whiteness of her body upon the great fourposter—the fourposter in which our children were begotten and born.

I wonder how Maisie feels about it all. She's so brave and fine that she'd never say how much it hurts . . . . I wonder how she feels now about the two-hundred-year-old sofa she says she's doing this to save. I'd rather have sold it to that dealer any day than have had that hard-voiced woman see into our bedroom. I'd rather have sold it, even though we'd felt we didn't want any stranger to sit on it and own it. Let that Yankee woman sit on it, if she chooses. Let them all sit on it and take it away, it and the prints and the china and Grandmamma's silver—so only we can have peace again. Anything rather than have that woman's hard voice within our home . . . . But where have they all gone to now? I can't seem to hear them any longer. . . . There's peace again for a while. . . . Peace again.

What's that coming now? Surely we've had enough for one day. But no, it's a bus, and it's filled with people. They must have made a mistake. They must be going to Natchez and have lost their way. They can't have meant to come in here. I must tell them which turning to take. . . . But they're getting out, all of them. They're getting out. Six—seven—eight—fourteen. Yes, fourteen of them. And all of them women. I can't stay here. I shan't know what to say. It must be Sam who's doing it, with that hat of his and the sweet smile on his face. But there are other people still inside there. It's so long since we've seen so many people we shan't know what to do. Oh, Maisie, where have you gone? I can't stand it here, all by myself.

"Yes, ma'm, this is the Delatrobe Place. Step this way, will you? Round there, to the bottom of the curved azalea walk, is the great avenue of live oaks, which is thought to be one of the finest in the whole of the Deep South. Not at all, ma'm, not at all. Delighted if you will all step this way."

It gets a little better after a time. But the redbird goes on singing and his song is drowned by strangers' chatter, and the moss is shaken by the bus as it passes. My silences have been taken from me.

The sun is sinking below the top of the live oaks. It flushes the white of the Cherokee roses and deepens the glow on the azaleas.

Sam will be back here soon. I told him to stay out there till the sun fell below the oaks. Why do I tremble like this, just because Sam's coming back to the house? I suppose I'm ashamed. Yes, that's it: I'm ashamed to meet him. I'm ashamed to hear how he has suffered today. Maisie and I, we can understand it all, but Sam can't. . . . There he is. That's his step coming up the avenue. I would know it anywhere. I've known it since I was the tiniest child. . . . But how quickly he is walking! And why is he swinging his stick like that, as though he were happy? And there's a broad grin on his face that I can't make out.

What's that he's saying? "All them ladies, Marse Will, they was good to see. Lord, Lord, Marse Will, hit were like the ol' ol' days in my chillun time, with the white folks comin' to the big house again. Ol' Sam he stood thar at the gates and he tuck off his hat and bowed to the ladies, and it was like life had come back here again. And life hit did crowd out all them hants and stillnesses, and Sam he jest lifted up his voice and praised the Lord God-A'mighty, because that folks was comin' again to visit Marse Will and Miss Maisie in the big house. Lord, Lord, Marse Will, Sam he's been so happy today that he can't hardly wait to go in to Mammie and celebrate."

It can't be true. I must be dreaming it. But there he is, hurrying to the house. He's hurrying in to see Mammie, and they're going to celebrate, those two. They're going to rejoice because they have heard voices again in this silent, mournful place. I ought to be glad. I ought to be glad in Sam's happiness. But I'm not. I'm lonely. I'm utterly, completely lonely. I thought he would understand. I supposed he knew. I hoped he'd hate those hard voiced women. But he has forsaken me and betrayed me, and I am left alone. . . . There he is, shouting in his joy, while I sit here in the gathering dusk, alone with my ghosts. Oh, Sam, Sam, Sam! How could you? How could you?

TOBACCO

**I** WONDERED if he had any idea of the drama of tobacco as he flung his half-finished cigarette thoughtlessly into the ash tray. The smoke rose in a straight thin column of blue. "Surely," I wanted to say to him, "surely, if you knew what went into the making of that one cigarette you would be forced to feel respect for it. You would finger it with care. You would look at it with wonder." And I found myself wishing for the magician's power, that I might use this thin straight column of smoke as an enchantment. I would curve it around him, and envelop him, this businessman, so that he might hear in his ears, louder than the New York traffic, the cries and tumult of the tobacco market, and live the night-long vigils before the flue-curing barns. Could I but bewitch him to revelation, I would transport him to the endless days of fierce heat in the tobacco fields of North Carolina, with the farmers worming the great leaves that would else be consumed in the hours between sunup and sundown. I would make him watch the tobacco plant with anxiety, for blue mold, and Granville wilt, and black shank, knowing that bread and meat and clothing were the hostages given to these blights. I would make him sleep at night in the great markets, boots for his pillow, an old patchwork quilt his covering, upon a truck for a bed, that he might be in time for the auction next morning. For the farms lie far from tobacco cities, and sales will not wait. I would—Oh, but could he stand it, this businessman? As I wonder, he has tossed another half-finished cigarette into the ash tray, and the smoke now rises in two straight columns into the air. Perhaps there is enough potency here, from the smoke of two cigarettes, to bewitch him. The noise of the night traffic of New

York seems, even as I think this, to be changing, and above the roar of the taxicabs I can hear, surely, an unmistakable bubbling sound.

Is it some prehistoric ceremonial dance that has come down through the ages? I feel here the magic of primitive man, and then suddenly I am in the Moenkopi Desert, watching the Niman Ka-china Dance of the Hopi Indians with their medicine man. He is a medicine man, if ever there was one, this auctioneer, and it is strange to the eye that he should be dressed in the ordinary clothes of the people of today. He sways and dances, in an ecstatic swoon, the strangest combination of rhythm and vulgarity. In appearance he is like a tout at the races, and against the grace of Negro porter and packer he has additional coarseness. Yet there is about him the inevi-table beauty of complete abandon. I watch him now, so drunk with self-created excitement that unconsciously he half closes his eyes as he waves his hands around and points and shakes throughout his entire body. This is no peripheral rhythm; this comes from the core of the man. Suppose it even to have started consciously, the result of training in a school of tobacco auctioneers, this self-intoxication is now surely authentic. But were it not, I must feel respect, for it is such complete artistry he has mastered, to look so effortless. Gazing upon this artist before me, I remember being told by one of the leading auctioneers that it takes from five to eight years for one of his profession to hit his prime. He must learn to pitch his chant in a medium key, that he may relax by raising or lowering that key. "When I'm feeling good," he said, "when I'm feeling good you can hear me across the warehouse."

"Twenny-one dollar bid twenny one-one-one-one—'n' hoff—'n' hoff—'n' hoff—'n' two—twenny-two dollar bid—twenny-two-two-two . . ." The auctioneer's hand darts around like a bird, as the words bubble out of one corner of his coarse mouth. He throws his head well back each time he knocks out a pile, and as the sale goes on his clothes drip with sweat, and his necktie swings limp and wet.

This sense of a ceremonial dance persists. Looking at the long lines of buyers, and at the way the figures bend down at the same moment, to examine the tobacco, and draw upright, in complete unison, it seems to me that this dance motif runs through all concerted work. Haymaking, harvesting, corn shucking, puddling in the steel mills—where men are gathered together to work, it is on a base of rhythmic movement.

Down one row and up the next the procession passes, the auctioneer stepping half sideways, half backwards, and his chanting might be the intoning of a priest, with the buyers as acolytes. But they lift a hand, or an eyebrow, or they twist a mouth, these buyers, and the auctioneer, watching each man, registers every flicker. The entire labor of a year changes ownership so swiftly, so barely perceptibly, that the ritual of the sale bewilders me. For the speed is set. Three hundred and sixty piles ahead stands a notice: "Sale due here 10:00 A.M." Within one hour these piles must be sold.

Throughout the day the sale goes on, and each person in this pageant knows his part and plays it ably. Auctioneer and farmer, peddler and sidewalk preacher, beggar and ticket marker, bookman and clipman, packer, floor laborer and "pinhooker": each is sure of his cues and his lines in the great drama of tobacco. But in all dramas there are villains and heroes—villains and heroes who may not even appear upon the stage, but without whom the drama could not exist. So, behind this noisy performance there lurks the dark green tobacco worm, larva of one of the hawk moths, instinct with perception for the tenderest, greenest leaves, voracious and unconquerable but by death, beautiful with its oblique stripes of black and white and the long "horn" at its tail end. And in league with the tobacco worm stalks the grasshopper, cutting the great leaves, while in attendance are the molds and wilts and rots that make the tobacco farmer's life a thirteen-month year of humble fear, and cause him to love the leaf with great care, as a mother cherishes a delicate child.

But there is, too, the hero of the drama, and its name is heat: heat from the time the seed is sown in virgin soil on the sunny side of a hill, under the stretched white cheesecloth that turns tobacco country into a land of sudden white clouds dropped to earth from the skies. Heat even before the sowing of the seed, when the farmers burn off the seedbeds with piles of brush and wood, and the February countryside in Kentucky glows with fires at night, and through the biting cold the women bring bowls of hot soup to their men. Heat for the raising of the crop, and the fierce sun of the Carolinas burns the fields, and light shines on the tobacco leaves, and farmers watch the plants for blight and mold, knowing the sun to be their true friend. Heat for the harvesting of the crop, and the negro primers sweat in the blistering fields, while the women loopers search in vain for shade beneath the small peach trees at the edge of the field. Heat for the flue-curing, and the great logs of oak and hickory and pine feed the fires in the tobacco barns day and night, and men sleep on straw pallets or primitive beds, that they may tend the fires that cure their crop.

And so, as I watch the auctioneer dancing up one row and down the next, thinking with amusement of the song of my childhood, "Up the middle and down again," I know that this market is but the one spectacular moment in a year-long struggle, and I see tired men after their vigils in the flue-curing barns and sleepy-eyed families starting for the market in the cold mists of dawn. I sit with old Jo Strong, and the rosy flames from the fire illumine the seventy-five-year-old man with his high cheekbones and the smooth pink skin to his face. He chews a new piece of tobacco every half-hour or so, at the same time that he slides a new log of a tree into the fire. His store teeth are stained yellow with this chewing tobacco, his gold-rimmed glasses sparkle in the glow from the flames as each new log catches alight. We sit through the long hours of darkness, and the night air of North Carolina is cool and sweet after the heat of the curing barn, where the temperature today is up to one hundred and fifty degrees and the smell of the drying tobacco sap chokes the throat and makes the eyes smart. But this barn now is Jo Strong's

last curing of the season. Though it be his poorest leaves, the tips, yet he has a tender care for the yellowing hands that hang upon the sticks from the rafters within the barn. As he talks to me about tobacco, I am infected by his excitement, and finger the curing leaves with the same love. "They're like silk, like satin," he murmurs, "they're so pretty—dappled yellow along the centre vein, and brown on the outside edges. They're soft as silk, they are."

He yawns, and turns for the long wooden rake, that he may shake himself awake by clearing the accumulation of cinders.

"I'm glad you're here with me tonight," he says, "for I suppose it must be my years tellin' on me. I used to be able to prime by day and watch at the curin' barns by night and never seem to want for sleep; but now it seems that my eyes get heavy before I know where I am, and I don't never dare even to lie down on that bed of mine over there, lest I fall asleep. I lost a barn once, when I was a little bitty trick of a thing. Thinkin' to be clever, I tried to push it, and never shall I forget the way that barn flamed up as it caught fire, and before you could hardly know what had happened there was nothin' left but a great black charred mass, and the trees around cracklin' and burnin'. And ever since then, over all these years, nobody can't make me lie down to sleep—no, not even if it were but for a few minutes. There's some as holds great all-night parties, with fiddles and chicken stew and women around. But not for me. If ever I'm tempted to any of that nonsense I say to myself: 'Jo Strong, you remember that flamin' barn with the great scarlet and crimson tongues of fire leapin' up to the very heavens as though it were the Day of Judgment, and don't you have anything to do with all that!' Now the color of these leaves is about fixed and I'll have to be bringin' the heat up to about a hundred and ninety degrees, for killin' it out, so as the stems will dry out. And then, if this weather goes on and we don't have no rain I'll have to sprinkle the floor with water when I open the doors and ventilators, so as to bring the tobacco in order, and make it pliable enough to be handled. If you're around here tomorrow I'll show you the pack house where we take it for a few days, before we grade it. Ever see tobacco bein' graded?"

But before I can answer him he has gone on talking.

"Do you see that rosy glow over there, between those trees? That's Tim Kelly's barns. He's got a right dandy crop this year, he has. And I tell you what, there isn't anythin' more pretty to me in the whole world than the rosy glow of a tobacco barn at night, in the days of curin', with that rosy glow dotted all over the countryside of North Carolina, like a garden of flowers, and the air filled with the sweet scent of wood smoke. Do you smell it right now, as the little wind blows down through the openin' in the trees? They can say what they like about pretty women and the beauties of nature, but give me a barn at night with the warm glow of the fire and the scent of hickory smoke, and the sound, when you listen carefully, of the crackle of the wood from the fires of all the tobacco barns around, jest as if it were big nuts dropped to the ground off a tree by great squirrels."

"But the tobacco barns themselves," I interrupt. "You haven't said what you think about them; for I think they are as beautiful as any buildings that man ever made." And I thought again of my delight in the shapes of the tobacco barns, the first time I had ever seen them. And I remembered the rows of barns in the snow, with the bright-colored advertisements pasted on their soft grey weatherworn wooden beams, and the dignity of their structure, unconfused by unnecessary embellishments. In my mind I placed them alongside corncribs in Maryland, great brown thatched barns in England, and deep-eaved farm buildings in the Austrian Tyrol; yes, and alongside, too, the curve of the old prairie schooner, or of the primitive wooden plow, or of all honest, earth forms that have been built with integrity and for the use of men. And so now, sitting out against this tobacco barn in North Carolina, I looked at the austere form against the night sky and at the way the trees sprung out from among these barns and, looking at the scene about me, I felt happy in its rhythm.

But Jo Strong is not listening. He has lifted a great log of hickory from the pyramid of fuel that stands beyond the far end of the barn and is carrying it toward the glowing fire. With a heave he slides it into the furnace and the flames catch it in their embrace.

"But don't you think it's better to let the tobacco dry out naturally?" I ask him, knowing that I venture upon a dangerous subject. For there is a strong rivalry between the flue-curing and the barn-curing farmers. And perhaps it is not by accident that Jo Strong does not seem to hear me. I remember the fanaticism of Ed Turner, in southern Maryland, and in my mind I follow him to the great red barn where the tobacco hangs. He opens the tall thin doors of his barn and strokes the tobacco that is curing there. "It stands to reason," he says, caressing the yellowing leaves, "It stands to reason that tobacco is better when it is cured slowly, by Nature, in a barn. Here in southern Maryland—just as they do down there in the mountains of North Carolina, or in Kentucky—here we cut the whole tobacco plant off, and the sweetness of the sap drains down into the leaves. And if you think of this, and of how we take off all the suckers so that the leaves shall be strong in flavor, you'll see that our way is better."

He has taken me round to the main door of the great barn, and now he leads me in, while he goes on talking.

"You start by crowning the top of the barn," he says, pointing to the high roof of this cathedral-like building, "and then you hang the barn right down—hang the sides down first, so as to keep the aisle open as long as you can."

It is strange, after living among the "hands" of tobacco in the Old Bright Belt of North Carolina to come here to these barns filled with hanging plants. Lying at my side I see the metal spear that is fixed to the end of a stick, to split the thick tobacco stalk as it is straddled on a pole. Looking at it, I realize the wide variety of craftsmanship there is in the raising and harvesting of tobacco, and I see the yellowish green fields on the mountain sides, so steep that it would seem that the crop might tumble. Mules draw the cut tobacco to the little weather-worn barns on flat wooden sleighs, and in some places the thick stalks are truly sun-cured, as they hang on rafters outside the barns, upon the hillsides. There is an intimacy about this particular tobacco harvest, where the crop is grown chiefly for the use of the farmers themselves. As the mountain people have a vegetable patch, and sorghum for their sweetening, so,

when all else is attended to, the one-horse farmers turn their minds to growing tobacco, and here there is none of the anguish and concern of the man whose entire livelihood depends for the whole year upon a battle against hornworm and hail, frost and blue mold. Bit by bit, as September comes around, the patches of sharp yellowish green upon the mountain sides, those patches that seem to be illumined by an unseen sun even when the sky is covered with clouds, they are so bright against the softer colors around them, these squares and rectangles of ripening tobacco change shape as a few rows are cut today, and another few rows tomorrow, and it doesn't really matter very much when they are harvested so long as it is done before the first frosts. Tobacco here, in the mountains, is treated casually. It is not the exacting master that it is in the real tobacco country, where the farmers are duly humble before its vagaries and, even after half a lifetime of raising the crop, will still say in all seriousness that they don't know anything, really, about tobacco.

And remembering this, I watch children worming and suckering through the heat of summer, and the small hands are sticky with the tobacco gum. I see them dropping the plants along the ridges, into the holes made for them in the ground with a pointed stick. I see tobacco being topped, and leaves watched for mold and blight. I sit with a small boy on the edge of a plant bed in South Carolina, in early spring, and we have drawn the cheesecloth to one side and, gazing upon a green lake of young tobacco, thick like duckweed upon a pond, we know that these small seedlings hold the power to bind us to this hot earth throughout the blazing months of summer, and that there will be for us no freedom until they have grown tall and strong and have been primed and graded and packed and sold. And I look, too, upon seed heads tied in a paper bag, and it is as though these solitary plants held some of the pride of a stallion; for they seem to know how bountifully they serve posterity.

But the July sun blazes upon the tobacco fields of North Carolina, and priming the lugs has begun. The color of the green leaves is a foil to the rich black of the primers' skin, and seems to cast a blue bloom upon the sweating flesh. Everything shines in the terrific heat, and over the great stretching fields there is no shade. Between the rows of tobacco slide the mule-drawn drakes, like narrow ships upon a mighty ocean. And on each side of the drake, just in front of the mule, moves a colored primer, bending, stooping to left and right, and endlessly to left and right, across the length of the blazing field in the blinding light as he primes the lugs. With his right hand he picks, and in the curve of his left arm he holds the leaves, their stems all one way, like a bunch of flowers that has been gathered in a garden. The mule pulls the drake forward a few steps, and into the vessel made of wood and sacking, the narrow ship that crosses this shining green ocean, up and down the rows, up and down till the edge of the field has been reached, into the drake are laid the great bundles of primed ripe leaves.

The August sun dallies in the sky above our heads, and the body leaves are ripe. The heat is frightening. Thankfully we follow the filled drake into the frugal shade of the peach tree, at the far end of the field, where two colored women empty the leaves from the drake and loop them swiftly, deftly, with thin string, to the stick across the "horse." A small Negro boy waits by their side, to carry the strung stick to its fellows upon the ground. They are in the shade of the peach tree, these two colored women, but even here the heat beats upon them, and nowhere is there any movement in the air. Beyond, in the small wood, among the pine trees and the gums, the tobacco farmer watches his barn, and within the darkness of that barn, where there is no sun, the thermometer hanging upon the wall registers a hundred and seventy degrees. He is killing out his tobacco, and heat will attend him into the night, when the relentless sun will have sunk below the edge of the fields and the air will have grown less fierce. Day or night, the farmer now is at the service and the command of heat.

"Ever seen tobacco bein' graded?" Jo Strong had not waited for

my answer, or I could have told him of the shed at the back of the barns where the Negro sat through the heat of September, binding up hands of tobacco. And the lugs and cutters and tips are graded, and the extra-good leaves are used as wrappers. I watch while he wraps the hand of tobacco with a leaf, so that the sheaf of twenty or thirty leaves is bound tight at the stem end to the size of a fifty-cent piece, and gaze at him as the hands are hung onto the four-foot stick, ready for placing on the truck. And as I look at these sticks, hung with the golden leaves, soft like silky suède, I see a farmer and his wife, with their big family of children, loading a truck overnight, that early next morning, perhaps even before dawn, the farmer may take the precious harvest to the market and by the slightest raising of some unknown buyer's eyebrows, turn the long hours and months of heat in the fields, the sleepless nights of vigil in the curing barns, the winter days of chopping wood for the firing of the furnaces, into a handful of dirty paper bills. As the farmer's wife looks at the loaded truck, all carefully tucked in with her discarded quilts, she sees before her eyes a washing machine and new shoes for young Ernest, and if luck comes their way this year, the set of mahogany bedroom furniture that she has had her eye on in a store window in Durham over many weeks.

And so, as I listen to the gurgling, bubbling chant of the auctioneer, and follow the procession of buyers, who bend and lift the hands of tobacco from the baskets, as I watch this dance of the tobacco market, this noisy, dust-filled market like a huge cathedral where a priest intones, as I swerve from the path of the Negro porters with their coats tied round their waists so that they shall not be stolen, the pageant of tobacco passes before me, with heat and work in the shadeless tobacco fields over the long months of summer, and the ravages of worm and damp and mold. I see tired-eyed farmers, and little children with sticky hands, and colored men with backs that ache from ceaseless bending, bending, bending, as they prime the lugs in the July sun.

Night falls, and the great market building fills for tomorrow's sale. In at the entrance of the building drive trailers and trucks. They throw mighty shadows behind them and the Negro packers merge into the darkness as they lift the sticks of tobacco hands from the trucks and lay them in the ordered pattern upon the baskets made of torn oak strips. Lights hang from the great building and catch the glisten of sweat on the Negroes' faces and glow on the gold of the tobacco, or sparkle upon the sprays that dampen the piled baskets along the aisles. Negro figures bend low as they cover these dampened baskets with stretches of canvas, and the tumult of gaiety in the streets beyond this house grows louder, enticing into the tobacco town farmer and porter. Timid wives may warn their men, but the spell of the town is already upon them, and they drift out to the fiddlers and the shooting galleries, the beer and the women. . . . I wander round in the dark empty building, and suddenly I come upon a man asleep. He lies on a truck, and under his head he has placed his boots. Over him is the old torn quilt that had protected his crop. I look more closely at him. He is a young white farmer, and there is exhaustion in his face; but sleep draws him back to childhood, and I am moved by the pathos of his helplessness. If you only knew, I want to tell him, if you only knew, you are the hero of this drama, the central figure—you who have plowed and sowed and wormed and suckered and primed. Those hands that lie helpless in sleep may be hard and horny and stained, but it is they that have filled the coffers of the rich.

The young white farmer stirs in his sleep, and, ashamed to have been watching him, I slip away. But I walk from the waiting building with triumph; for I have seen the figure upon whom all this centres, and without whom it could not exist.

SATURDAY IN
COURT HOUSE SQUARE

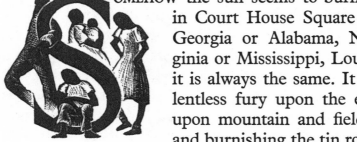OMEHOW the sun seems to burn down more fiercely in Court House Square than anywhere else. Georgia or Alabama, North Carolina, Virginia or Mississippi, Louisiana or Tennessee, it is always the same. It beats today with relentless fury upon the entire earth; it beats upon mountain and field, bleaching the soil and burnishing the tin roofs of the cabins to a glaring silver. It beats upon the shadeless dirt roads that draw people to the town, drying the surface till each mule cart and each automobile throws up a screen of dust. It beats upon grazing cattle and trudging Negroes, till the animals pant as they seek the stingy shadow of a fence, and the sweat on the bodies of the black men dries on their backs even while the dripping shirts stick to their skin. But as we reach the outskirts of the country town, where the squalid cabins of the colored quarter huddle and yards are crowded with mules waiting to be shod, the air is filled with the hot smell of scorching hooves from the mules' feet and confined by cabin and fence. On through the tributary streets we make our way, past the Baptist Church of the Wholly Sanctified and the small textile factory that supports the town, and the heat grows greater with each step we take. Shabby automobiles, tumble-down jalopies, dust-covered wagons and trucks edge the roads, and the crowds upon the sidewalks flow more and more slowly as they thicken.

At last we have reached Court House Square. Guardian, sentinel, avenger stands the Court House itself, hot red brick, pompous and unbending. Before the columned entrance, at the top of the steps, the statue of an unimportant hero holds out his cool stone hand to the milling masses beneath him. And according as you be Negro or tenant farmer, moonshiner or gangster, po' white, share cropper or moneyed aristocrat, so does that outstretched hand vary its message, till it can beckon to the electric chair or the jail, or welcome to the company of the elect. The Court House stands in the centre of the square, stern, condemning, and protecting.

But if the crowds that clump upon the sidewalks of Court House Square feel anything about this central power that ultimately controls their lives, it is not in their conscious minds. This, here, today, is the apex of their week. Alone upon a farm in the mountains, chopping cotton in the blazing heat of the far-stretching field, hoeing between the rows of corn, dropping tobacco plants along the ridge, whether it be in the Carolinas or Georgia, Alabama, Virginia, Mississippi, or Tennessee, there is always a road that leads out from the farm among the mountains, the cotton field, the cornfield, the tobacco patch, and always this road leads on Saturday across the blazing heat to Court House Square.

For man must meet with his fellows. He must weave his single strand into the whole pattern of life. So rich in color, so intricate in weave, so throbbing with human emotion is this pattern in Court House Square, that it is almost as though one can put one's hand upon it and feel the violence of the beat of its huge pulse. And wandering among these people, these leaning, lounging men in their blue jeans, these gossiping women in their clean shabby prints, these Negroes with their look of unrest, these small thin children with flaxen hair and bare feet, I know that behind the ordinary exteriors, the seemingly quiet eyes, surge unsuspected passions, and hates and loves that consume, and that ingrained habit alone controls these bodies as they stroll the sidewalks of Court House Square. But surely, I feel, it is something of the emotion of this complicated pattern that adds to the oppressive heat. Enclosed within these four

147

blocks of buildings, here is the distillation of intensely felt life drawn at one moment into this small square well from the countryside around. This that I watch is no diluted existence. If I could only know what is happening inside them, I find myself wishing. If I could only see within the mean face of that redheaded man over there, leering at the thin young girl who is carrying so many packages, or of that pale child in the plaid cotton dress who hurries toward the corner by the post office, or of the tired-eyed old woman with the concave chest and the protruding belly that must unwillingly have borne so many children.

But from the corner by the post office, in front of the antique shop, I hear the sound of a man singing. I follow the sound and find myself on the edge of a little clump of people surrounding a mountain singer. He sits under a tree, and upon a patch of grass, in a circle, squat his listeners. The pale child in the plaid dress is there before me. I join the listeners on the ground, and as I look about me, I notice that most of us are women. Next to me sits a fat, middle-aged woman with a soft look in her eyes. She calls to the mountaineer.

"Sing me, 'I'm thinkin' of my blue eyes'," she begs, and, turning to me, she adds: "I did use to sing that song nineteen years ago, I did."

The mountaineer picks his guitar and sings the song; her eyes grow yet softer, and she places her hand in mine, in an unstated comradeship of emotion.

And now the ugly old woman on the far side of me calls the tune, and as the romantic mountain man in the check flannel shirt and the bright blue trousers and the great black felt hat sings her choice, tears trickle down the dirty lined face in pale rivulets and fall upon the old black coat.

"Now then, young man, those songs aren't near as short as you make them," she orders him. "You don't pick long enough, you don't. When my boy did use to sing that song to me many, many years ago—long before your pappy was born—he did sing more verses to it. I know, for I know them."

And the mountaineer laughs as he obeys her bidding.

I am surrounded this morning by an orgy of recollected emotions. It is no wonder that the bums on the outer edge of this clump slink away as though they did not belong. For this is a women's gathering, and the singer knows his public. Not until this evening will he produce his work songs and his cowboy songs. The men then will surround him and the music and the singing will rise into the air above the roar of the traffic.

But I find myself watching the pale little girl in the plaid cotton dress. During the singing of these romantic songs she has stood so close to the mountain man that I could scarcely see him, and upon her face there was a look of expectancy that almost scared me with its tenseness. Now, as there is a lull in the singing, shyly she tosses a hot nickel into the open guitar case, and, leaning towards him, whispers something in his ear. He nods, as though in league with her, and knocking his guitar as a fit beginning for his song, he sings her "Barnacle Bill the Sailor." I watch the pale child's face as she listens to the song, and it is transfixed with love; but there is something else in that face that worries me, and later in the morning, as I make friends with her and we sit side by side on the patch of grass, I learn her story and I understand.

"I always come each Saturday morning and get him to sing that song," she whispers to me. "My daddy loves it, and I love my daddy."

"But why does this mountaineer have to sing it then?" I ask her. "Why don't you get your daddy to sing it to you?"

"He can't exactly sing it to me," she explains quietly. "You see, he's in the State penitentiary." She pauses, and adds yet more quietly: "And I'll be a big girl when he comes out, for he'll be there nineteen more years. Last year, you see, he killed a man."

My heart gives a jolt in my chest. So this is how tragedy comes among us, quietly, simply, out from the mouth of this soft-faced pale child. I look about me at the women clumped on the grass, wondering what may lie hidden in their lives, too, behind the quiet faces.

But the mountaineer is telling his tall tales now, and laughter runs round the circle of listeners. They are threadbare tales, perhaps, but he tells them with such gusto that, for the moment, we believe that they truly happened to him. I listen to the tale of the grubbing hoe that was bitten by a rattler till it swelled large enough, so that he built himself a four-roomed house with the wood, only to find, one morning bright and early, as he went out to look at it under the coat of paint he had given it, that overnight the turpentine had taken the swelling out of the wood and the house had disappeared. As I 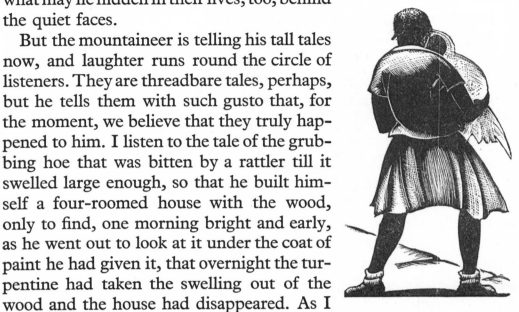 watch the excitement of his listeners I know that he satisfies a very real need. He is the sense of drama in the uneventful lives of these country people. Telling myself this, I smile at supposing their lives to be uneventful. But drama is only drama when it is experienced collectively, and at second hand, I decide. This, then, is what we need: to sit with our fellow men and watch the tragedies and comedies of life enacted by someone else. It is not dramatic tragedy to the Negress when her man slashes with a knife at the husband of his outside woman. Jesse Perrick does not boast of the drama in his life, because he has killed the man who tried to steal his still. Old Ollie may feel sorry for herself, but she is unaware that she epitomizes the tragedy of a mighty race problem. But let Jesse and Ollie and the Negro cotton chopper and the pale little child in the plaid cotton dress come to their Court House Square and hear some second-rate tale told with the touch of the artist by a mountain singer or story-teller, and they will thrill to the sense that they are truly living. This, then, is one of the secrets of the gathering together in Court House Square on a Saturday.

As I leave the mountain singer I work my way very slowly along the sidewalk, for the crowds thicken with each minute. It becomes Court House Square in the Alabama Black Belt, far away from any mountains, and the people on the streets wave like trees in a breeze. This is not a company of sunburnt, gangling farmers who loll lazily against store windows, or sit quietly on the ledge of the post-office building. This is a lilting, dancing crowd of colored people, driven almost crazy by the rhythm of the loud-speakers that bellow their blues from the main hotel and from the central drugstore. For the two rhythms meet and spar, and as the currents of sultry air come first from one way and then from another, so does one loud-speaker overpower its rival and control the dance steps of the colored people on the sidewalk. Feet slide and slither and twist and turn as they walk, and behinds, tightly encased in shiny black satin or transparent silk, wriggle and shake. Here is none of the sedate, introvert tragedy of the poor white, the mountain farmer. Here is a pouring out of the emotions, an uncontrolled excess of the senses that lies thick over everything. As one watches the seductive wriggles of the colored girls' behinds, and the slight lift to their thick, heavily reddened lips, one understands the answering light in the eyes of the young men. Heat over everything. Heat of the Alabama sun. Heat striking up from the cement sidewalks. Heat coming from dark young bodies that lilt to the radio. A slim Negro girl passes me in a tight black dress; on the front of her dress, blazoned upon one thigh, is sewn a great red heart. And as a lesson that their blood will not heed, a young child-mother totes her baby before her in her arms, the weight of the infant almost more than she can carry.

Across the street, in the Court House gardens, magnolia trees spread the scent of their heavy white blossoms upon the hot air, and mimosa trees are lavish in their perfumed bloom. For it is late May in Alabama, and Nature conspires to be served. In the shade of one of the mimosa trees, on the low stone ledge that bounds the Court House grounds, sits Aunt Becky, her great legs apart, her body streaming with sweat. The feathery-leaved branches of the mimosa are weighted down by old slips and panties, and by her side, in cardboard boxes, is littered a collection of old hats, shirts, dresses and brassieres. Half ashamed, the tall thin colored man waits while his girl searches in these boxes for a pair of pants, and he turns away as he sees her look next to the baby clothes in the case at the far side of Aunt Becky.

White shoes click on the hot sidewalks, and jewels upon throats and wrists catch the light of the Alabama sun and blind the eyes of the passers-by. Court House Square today sparkles and burns.

Georgia or Alabama, Virginia, the Carolinas, Mississippi, or Tennessee, this is the weekly liberation for mankind, under the very eye of the sentinel Court House.

Saturday in the tobacco country, and the farmers have money to spend, and furniture dealers do a roaring trade. Saturday in the Mississippi Delta, and cotton prices are low, and the pickers stand at street corners and swear. The old colored picker over there, by the peanut roasting store, is shouting to a friend about his miseries. "I honors my pains, I do," he bellows, "and nobody is going to get me that I don't honor them. And I tell you what, them what says we shouldn't moan, they don't know nothin'."

Saturday in Georgia, and the poor whites bring their families of flaxen-haired, barefooted children to town. Their feet are reddened by the native clay, their overalls patched and clean. They stand around the railroad station that lies at the back of Court House Square, waiting in little groups for the arrival of the trains. There may be nobody they know who will come by these trains, but it is people they will see, and the rush and the roar of the railroad terminus is good after six days of quietness, of quietness among the eroded red fields, with only the jangle of the mule's harness for company. . . . An unknown couple gets off by the next train; it must be father and daughter. The long, thin man with the big Adam's apple and deep-set eyes leans on the arm of the young girl by his side, the young girl, cadaverous-looking, with the cheap sparkling necklace and untidy hair that is ragged-edged beneath her shabby straw hat. They leave the station as though they find the flat smooth ground difficult to negotiate with their feet after the rough land that they are wont to tread. They look about them with fear in their eyes, as if they have landed in a hostile world. Under his arm the man carries a little parcel that he fingers tenderly. With a slouching walk they move away, followed by a host of inquiring eyes. They walk off the stage of our drama, and never shall we know what the man carries within that parcel, or where they have gone.

Saturday in Court House Square in Alabama, and Jesse Perrick forgets his loneliness in corn liquor, and Ollie finds that she "belongs." She is deep in conversation with an old colored crony whose face is tense with terror as she talks. I draw nearer, that I may overhear. "And me, as had made my livin' all my life, since my chillun time, rearin' and killin' chickens, and ever'thing went well until yesterday, when I looks up and there is the chicken debbil facin' me, as large as can be. And he had the debbil's head, and chicken's wings and webbed feet. And I tries to run away from him, and at last I manages to hide beneath one of his wings and I runs WITH him when he chases me. And do you know why he came to me like that?" The old crony puts her face so close to Ollie that I can scarcely hear what she is saying. Keenly I listen while she hisses: "Hit wasn't because I killed them chickens. Hit was because I LIKED killin' them."

I am swept away in an eddy of the crowd, and shall never know

153

what Ollie thought about it. But I carry with me the memory of a comfortable look on her face, as though, for this short while, she truly "belongs." She is back in her own world of primitive beliefs.

Saturday in Virginia, and I loiter in Court House Square among the colored people. Two old Negroes sit on the low wall that surrounds the Court House garden, deep in a religious discussion. I put my packages on the wall and wait, as though it were for a bus.

"Why, we're so fur deep in sin that hit would take the angels years and years to reach us these days from heaven," moans the lame old colored man. "Even prostolic man, back in Adam's day, is still marchin' to Zion, a long, long way beyond the furthest star."

"And hif'n the Lord God was angry with Moses in the days of Egypt, when the people of His'n did keep all His statues, how couldn't He be angry with us now, when we don't do nothin' but be wicked and childish and sinful?"

The second old man shakes his head and moans.

A third Negro has come and he settles himself on the wall at the far side.

"I tell you," he mumbles, "I tell you hit's real serious, this war is, when you think that there'll only be two of a kind left befo' hit's over, jest like in the days of Noah."

More friends join them, and the talk grows general. As I wander away I am sad within me to think of the mess we have made of their simple world.

But even the state of the world fails to stop their dark laughter.

Over in the barber shop, as they wait their turn, a clump of Negroes listens to the tale of a 'possum hunt.

"Ol' Uncle Nick—you remember him?—he were then about ninety years old, he were. But he did sure love his 'possum hunt, and hit grieved him sorely that he was gettin' too old and frail to go out with the others. Hit grieved him so badly that his family tuck that hickory chair he was so fond of from the po'ch and fixed it up with two bean poles through hit, so hit was like a sort of bed to take him in, and they, two of them, one in front and one behind, they did carry him in this bed to the hunt."

The clump of listeners has swelled, till they occupy most of the spare space in the barber shop. The story-teller continues:

"Ol' Uncle Nick, he were that happy he didn't jest know what to do, and when the dogs treed a 'possum he was excited with the rest. And they puts down Uncle Nick in his bed to wait while they cuts down the tree. But you folks know what happened?" With true artistry the Negro pauses, and the clump of listeners draws closer in, that it may not miss one word, one lift of the brow.

"Hit waren't no 'possum that the dogs had treed, but a b'ar. Yes, sir, a b'ar. And the men they all ran as fast as their legs could carry them till they was out of danger. And then, suddenly, they thinks of ol' Uncle Nick, bedridden, left behind thar alone in the bed, and they decides that hit hain't no good their goin' back for him now, fo' there jest wouldn't be no Uncle Nick left. So they continues on home. And when they reaches home thar, settin' on the porch, is Uncle Nick hisself."

Laughter fills the barber shop, till the colored people in the chairs try to turn their heads to see what is happening.

Saturday in North Carolina, and tomorrow is the great baptizing at the City of God in the Wilderness. The body of Dossie Rogers walks in Court House Square, but her spirit wanders far, for tomorrow she will be saved. She will stand on the river bank and sing, "Shall we gather at the river, the beautiful, beautiful river," and God will descend upon her like a dove, yes, in the form of a shining white dove that will nestle in her hair, her hair that she is just going to the beauty parlor to get fixed. And her mother has told her to put weights into the hem of her white dress, else it will float up around her waist as she descends into the water and the Reverend will have to poke it down with his cane, jest as it happened to her big sister last year, and she was so ashamed. And—but she is at the door of the beauty parlor, and as she vanishes from our sight she carries with her the vision of a shining dove.

Saturday in the mountains, and the people have trekked many miles from their homes in the far-off coves, bringing with them to the milling crowd in Court House Square serenity in their faces and dignity in their walk. They mix with these crowds, and everywhere is seen the uniform of the American worker, which is to be found whether on the land, or in the city, along the water front or from the factory; everywhere here are seen the overalls, the blue jeans—bright in color when they are new, soft and faded when they have faced the burning sun upon cotton field or corn land, dark in the creases that are shaded from the burning sun, loose upon the long limbs of the mountain man, the colored man, gay with labelled suspenders. They are the proud symbol of the man who works with his hands. And they predominate in Court House Square, for this is the workers' day, and the rest of the world keeps itself superior and remote.

All the bums of the neighborhood are here, clustered along the ledges of the Court House, in the shadow of the very power that they most fear. But there is no fear today as they laugh and talk and get drunk, for, gathered together as they are, they feel able to defy the cold stone statue that beckons from the top of the Court House steps. Up the hill an old mountaineer tunes his fiddle, and a crowd collects around him. "Looks like a corn shuckin' beginnin', or a log rollin' or sumpthin'," drawls the thin man at the far end of the ledge.

In the shabby, dust-covered cars that border the sidewalks sit wives with young children on their knees and great stacks of provisions heaped around them. A sunburnt farmer tosses his baby high in the air above him as he waits for his wife to open her dress; for it is feeding time. Ice-cream cones melt in the hot hands of small children and drip upon clean clothes and polished shoes. Women lean over the sides of the cars, gossiping to the young mothers within as they nurse their babies. This, today, is a rich tapestry of living, passionate in weave, with rough, tragic ends on the inner side, but a glow of colors in the strands. Obedient to the instinctive needs of man, these people have come together here under the pretext of marketing, even as the people in England, or in the small towns of the old France, or in Italy or Spain, or any country in the world that you might mention, obey the need to meet and merge their solitary lives into the common pool of mankind. Man needs to meet with man, before he goes back to the mountains and the lonely farm lands, to his isolated life of true, deep drama. But this drama that he lives is the one of which he is completely unaware. He does not see the grandeur of his own life or know that it is the fabric of all poetry and all song.

Saturday in Court House Square in Georgia or Alabama, Virginia, the Carolinas, Mississippi, Louisiana, or Tennessee: this, now, is our privilege to see man with all his lovable foibles and all his endearing needs. For he is the same the world over, lonely and insecure; and for sustenance during his week of labor he needs the reassurance of this merging with his fellow men, this offering of his single identity upon the communal altar of life.